Judging Lincoln

Yours truly
A. Lincoln—

Judging Lincoln

‹ঽ Frank J. Williams ঽ›

With a Foreword by Harold Holzer

and an Epilogue by John Y. Simon

Southern Illinois University Press
Carbondale and Edwardsville

Frontispiece: Robert M. Cole, photographer. Peoria, Illinois, ca. 1858. Signed photograph (10¾ × 9 inches), probably made during the Lincoln and Douglas senatorial campaigns, that portrays Lincoln at the apex of his political and legal careers in Illinois. From The Frank and Virginia Williams Collection of Lincolniana; photograph by Virginia Williams.

Library of Congress Cataloging-in-Publication Data

Williams, Frank J.
  Judging Lincoln / Frank J. Williams ; with a foreword by Harold Holzer ; and an epilogue by John Y. Simon.
    p. cm.
  Includes bibliographical references and index.
    1. Lincoln, Abraham, 1809–1865. 2. Political leadership— United States—History—19th century. 3. Character. I. Title.
  E457.2 .W69 2002
  973.7'092—dc21
  [B]
                                        2002018758

  ISBN 0-8093-2391-5 (cloth : alk. paper)

Printed on recycled paper. ♻

The paper used in this publication meets the minimum requirements of American National Standard for Information Sciences—Permanence of Paper for Printed Library Materials, ANSI Z39.48-1992.∞

For Virginia and my parents,
Natalie and Frank,
who have tolerated me and
Abraham Lincoln
all through the years

Contents

Contents

Illustrations

Illustrations

Illustrations

Foreword

DURING THE famous Illinois senatorial debates of 1858, challenger Abraham Lincoln liked to goad his opponent incumbent, Stephen A. Douglas, by referring to him by a name clearly meant in those days to disparage him: judge. With Lincoln, it was never "Senator Douglas." It was always "Judge Douglas." The old debate transcripts still fairly crackle with the subtle but disparaging inflection that Lincoln must have brought to the task of so teasing "the Little Giant."

It was not that Lincoln held the entire judiciary in disregard. In fact, he counted several judges as friends and political allies, among them David W. Davis, whom he would one day name to the United States Supreme Court. And Lincoln himself had served as a judge from time to time, presiding over the occasional case on the Illinois Eighth Judicial Circuit when preassigned jurists became unavailable.

But in 1858, Lincoln was also deep in a war of criticism against the Supreme Court's recent *Dred Scott* decision, which he believed emblematic of a Democratic Party conspiracy to nationalize slavery. Douglas huffed in reply that his rival was doing nothing less than "making war" on a decision made by the nation's highest tribunal. Lincoln disagreed.

In a stinging reply at the Quincy debate on October 13, Lincoln reminded his audience that Douglas himself had years earlier worked "to reverse a decision" of Illinois's own state supreme court, in the bargain winning the judgeship that Lincoln now enjoyed ridiculing. "Did he not go and make speeches in the lobby and show how it was villainous," Lincoln asked, "and did he not succeed in procuring the reorganizing of the court, and did he not succeed in sitting on the bench, getting his name of Judge in that way?" Clearly, being a judge was no certain avenue to respect where Lincoln was concerned.

John D. Whiting, [Lincoln and Douglas in Debate]. Undated. Oil painting, 23½ × 16 inches. This illustrator captured the great difference in height between Abraham Lincoln and Stephen A. Douglas. Harold Holzer, who published this image in his *Lincoln-Douglas Debates: The First Complete, Unexpurgated Text* (New York: HarperCollins, 1993), believes that the scene represents the debate at Ottawa, Quincy, or Alton, each of which occurred in a town square much like the one depicted here. From The Frank and Virginia Williams Collection of Lincolniana; photograph by Virginia Williams.

But then, Abraham Lincoln never knew Frank J. Williams. One suspects that if he had, Lincoln would have cheerfully referred to him as "judge," too—but without a whit of sarcasm.

On the other hand, Judge Williams—now Chief Justice Williams of the Rhode Island Supreme Court—certainly knows Abraham Lincoln. He has spent a lifetime not only studying Lincoln but doing his best to emulate him. Inspired by him as a student, Williams went on to practice law for the same number of years as Lincoln did a century earlier. He then won a place on the Rhode Island Superior Court and, from there, nomination by his governor and unanimous confirmation by his state legislature as the state's chief justice. Not even Lincoln ever won an election without a dissenting vote.

What is most extraordinary about Rhode Island's top jurist, however, is that throughout his long and busy career in the law (he has also attended a state constitutional convention and served as a town moderator in his "spare time"), he has managed to emerge as the country's most influential, successful, and popular Lincoln organizational leader. This I can say from firsthand experience, having served with him on the executive board of the Abraham Lincoln Association during a few of the nine years he led that group as president and enlarged the organization significantly. I am also a fellow director of the Ulysses S. Grant Association, which Judge Williams serves as president, too. And I am vice chair of the Lincoln Forum, the national organization that Judge Williams cofounded and has chaired since its inception, transforming it from a mere idea into a genuine national treasure: a true public forum on cutting-edge Lincoln scholarship, regularly made available to millions of viewers on C-SPAN.

Wherever he has served in the Lincoln sphere, in fact, Judge Williams has stirred interest, increased membership, built a loyal following, and fostered appreciation of Lincoln and his era. Both of us were honored in 2000 with appointments to the United States Abraham Lincoln Bicentennial Commission—his, a nomination from the Republican side of the aisle, mine from the Democratic. (Fortunately, we do not get along like Lincoln and Douglas did; in fact, we are the best of friends.) More great things might reasonably be expected from him as he responds to this latest challenge, and one would not be foolhardy to wager that he will exert a major influence on the celebration of Lincoln's two hundredth birthday in 2009.

But that is not all. Somehow, Frank J. Williams has concurrently built yet another avocational career over the past twenty years: that of a highly effective, thoroughly original, and remarkably peripatetic writer and lecturer on the Lincoln theme. He has delivered major papers at all the important Civil War and Lincoln conferences. He remains a staple at the regular symposia at Lincoln Memorial University and Robert Todd Lincoln's "Hildene," and in one recent year delivered two of the most prestigious Lincoln lectures in the entire field: the R. Gerald McMurtry Lecture at the Lincoln Museum in Fort Wayne, and the annual Watchorn Lecture at the Lincoln Shrine in Redlands, California. Those admirers who lack the presumption to entertain thoughts of *being* Frank Williams might still aspire merely to be his travel agent!

Many of his lectures have appeared in print before, in journals and in important collections of the papers and proceedings of scholarly conferences. What has been lacking—until now—is a single volume of his best work. Its arrival promises to reveal, to a wider audience than ever, his highly original perspective, his gift for comprehensible analysis of complex legal and political issues, and his relentless curiosity about the deepest, often least studied, aspects of Abraham Lincoln's life and career. Lincoln scholars used to be referred to as "authorities." It is a title one cannot help but feel rests comfortably on Williams's shoulders: He is an authoritative figure in every sense of the phrase.

"The leading rule for the lawyer, as for the man of every other calling, is *diligence*," Lincoln wrote around 1850. No lawyer—and no Lincoln scholar—has been more diligent over the past quarter century than Frank J. Williams. He has worked tirelessly to foster appreciation for American history and has demanded the highest standards of scholarship and research from himself and from others. He has devoted time, energy, intellectual ability, and that rarest of gifts, leadership, to the two causes that have shaped his life: to paraphrase Lincoln, reverence for the laws and reverence for the past.

These pages contain the fruits of his labors. They will nourish the Lincoln literature.

> Harold Holzer
> Vice President for Communications
> Metropolitan Museum of Art
> Cochairman
> U.S. Abraham Lincoln Bicentennial Commission

Acknowledgments

First and foremost I credit my closest Lincoln friend, Harold Holzer, author and cofounding vice chairman of the Lincoln Forum, for suggesting that I do this book of essays. He even suggested the title, read the manuscript, and provided the foreword. I am deeply indebted to Michael Vorenberg of Brown University, author of the definitive study on the Thirteenth Amendment, *Final Freedom: The Civil War, the Abolition of Slavery, and the Thirteenth Amendment,* for his close read of this manuscript and excellent suggestions for revising and improving the essays. My fellow Vietnam veteran, John ("Sgt. Rick") Stetter, director of Southern Illinois University Press, fulfilled his early promise to do this book. He assigned Elizabeth Brymer as my editor. She could not have been more accommodating, patient, and supportive. Thanks, too, to all at SIUP for their team effort. And what would an author do without a good copy editor? So my gratitude goes to Elaine Durham Otto for her questions and suggestions. My friend John Y. Simon, executive director of the Ulysses S. Grant Association and a Lincoln scholar in his own right, supported this project with enthusiasm and verve. I am grateful for his epilogue and constructive criticism. Marilyn Penney, aka Miss Moneypenny, was indispensable in preparing several drafts of the manuscript. My friend, coauthor, and coeditor, William D. Pederson, director of the International Lincoln Center at Louisiana State University in Shreveport, provided his usual efficient editorial assistance. My administrative assistant, Donna Petorella, assisted me on her own time by typing many of the essays when they were first published. I was also aided by two distinguished catalogers of The Frank and Virginia Williams Collection of Lincolniana: David M. Rich, cataloger extraordinaire, who has been with the collection for twenty years, and Alfred Calabreta, who continues to catalog everything else—prints, philately, numismatics, broadsides, photographs, paintings, and ephemera. Finally, I want to acknowledge and thank all of my friends in the Lincoln "family" who have supported and inspired me over the years. Of course, any errors are solely my responsibility.

Introduction

THE DAWN OF THE twenty-first century seems an appropriate time to reevaluate ourselves both as a nation and as a people: where we have been, where we are, and where we might be going. And for me, Abraham Lincoln remains the central figure of the American experience, past, present, and future. I began collecting books about Lincoln fifty years ago. Then I became an organizational leader, first in the Lincoln Group of Boston, then the Abraham Lincoln Association, and now the Lincoln Forum. As I became more immersed in studying our sixteenth president, I began writing about him and his leadership legacy. Growth of my interest in Lincoln paralleled my quarter century practice as a lawyer and now as a judge. In my judicial role, I have come to appreciate more than ever that citizens must make judgments daily, just as I do. In a broad sense, as political theorists remind us, democratic politics means making choices—it is unavoidable. As a collector, I must decide what to buy within budget restraints. As an organizational leader, I have had to decide how to reach out to others who share my interests. As a writer, I must decide which aspects of Lincoln to research. These essays, written over twenty-five years and updated for this volume, reflect my choices and approach to Lincoln.

My first essay, "Abraham Lincoln, Our Ever-Present Contemporary," was based on my years of writing an annual Lincolniana article for the *Journal of the Abraham Lincoln Association,* the *Lincoln Herald,* and *Lincoln Lore.* I have observed the fluctuating interest in Lincoln, both domestically and internationally. Notwithstanding the relativism espoused by some recent scholars, I am convinced that Lincoln's leadership style is one of the greatest gifts of American democracy to the world.

Presidential scholars unanimously rank Lincoln as the greatest president. One sign of his enduring influence is that more books (estimated at seventeen thousand), journals, newsletters, and organizations have been devoted

James Montgomery Flagg, title unknown. Undated. Oil painting, 47¾ ×
26¼ inches. This artist and illustrator, who created the Uncle Sam "I
Want You" recruiting poster for both world wars, often painted himself
as Abraham Lincoln because of his physical resemblance to the sixteenth
president. This painting has been described as showing Lincoln waiting
for news from the second battle of Bull Run; it certainly demonstrates
Lincoln's intensity of emotion as he waits nervously for reports from the
front. From The Frank and Virginia Williams Collection of Lincolniana;
photograph by Virginia Williams.

to preserving his legacy than have been created for any other president. Lincoln enthusiasts in the United States need to work with our friends overseas so that the entire world "gets right" with Lincoln.

The next essay, "'A Matter of Profound Wonder': The Women in Lincoln's Life," attempts to define the personal character of a political leader. How does he or she treat those nearest at hand: as subordinates or as equals? This is particularly important with Lincoln, since most still revere him as the Great Emancipator. Did he practice what he preached, or was he an opportunistic politician? My research suggests that Lincoln truly liked people, and they responded in kind, even though he was not the typical glad-handed politician. He may have achieved wealth and prominence as a railroad lawyer, but he recognized and appreciated the role of his stepmother, his wife, and other women in his development. The politician-statesman who would write about the universal family of man was grounded in a family of friends. Aristotle long ago noted that friendships are the best kind of relationships, since they are based on the notion of equality. Lincoln's behavior epitomized Aristotle's intellectual insight.

The next six essays focus on the broad challenge of classifying Lincoln's leadership. Was he autocrat or democrat, conservative or liberal, idealist or Machiavellian? The answer, of course, is that he reflected a bit of each. However, in the broadest sense, he was able to reconcile America's ideals with its practices. He became America's Socrates. Just as Socrates used his powerful intellect to put Athens on trial during his own political trial, Lincoln used the Civil War to put the United States on trial at the same time that his own leadership was being tested. The sectional crisis forced Lincoln to transform himself from a local Whig into a national Republican who drew a philosophical line at the extension of slavery into the national territories. "Abraham Lincoln: Commander in Chief or 'Attorney in Chief'?" attempts to demonstrate that when Lincoln assumed the executive role for which he lacked experience, he relied on finely tuned political instincts based on his legislative experience and not just the narrow legalistic approach one might expect from a lawyer.

The initial, extraconstitutional presidential steps he used to address the nation's internal crisis elevated him above hack politicians, yet his actions required congressional approval, which would prevent him from succumbing to the allure of dictatorship. In "Abraham Lincoln and Civil Liberties,"

I discuss how easy it is to condemn Lincoln as an authoritarian leader if one fixates on the suspension of habeas corpus. However, that abridgement must be placed within the context of the Civil War. More important, Lincoln insisted that the 1864 presidential election be held despite his belief that he would lose.

In "Abraham Lincoln: The President and George Gordon Meade — An Evolving Commander in Chief," I note how Lincoln's political fate depended on winning the war. Despite being plagued with a series of unsuccessful generals, Lincoln's treatment of his military leaders and his belated willingness to learn the art of war, which Machiavelli saw as crucial for a Prince, reflects favorably on the president's character. He could lose his temper over incompetence. But, unlike tyrants, he checked his anger.

In "A View from the Field," I discuss how Lincoln faced both political and military competition. He placed his major competitors in his cabinet and eventually fired the general most admired by soldiers in the Union army, then restored him temporarily. Through his actions (continually visiting the troops) and persuasive writings, Lincoln won over the troops as he would the general public. And, of course, he was more than willing to allow the soldiers to vote in the 1864 election. Despite his tenuous hold on the presidency, Lincoln engaged in every possible political maneuver to win reelection.

His use of Machiavellian tactics to pass the Thirteenth Amendment supported his ultimate aim. Lincoln's commitment to holding a democratic election in time of war earned for him recognition as democracy's greatest democrat. "The End of Slavery" discusses the fact that Lincoln was not an idealist but a practical politician with principles. Just as the framers of the U.S. Constitution thought it prudent to hedge their bets on the world's first large experiment in self-governing by giving the Supreme Court authority to curb the excesses of democracy, Lincoln was willing to cut corners to institutionalize the Thirteenth Amendment, especially when his reelection seemed unlikely.

Lincoln died as his dramatic trial was concluding, but his legacy endures. This nation withstood the ordeal of a civil war largely thanks to Lincoln's principled leadership.

"Warrior, Communitarian, and Echo: The Leadership of Abraham Lincoln, Winston Churchill, and Franklin D. Roosevelt" offers a qualitative comparative case study of the three political leaders, Abraham Lincoln,

Introduction

Franklin Delano Roosevelt, and Winston Churchill in order to make further distinctions about Lincoln. Historians rank Roosevelt as America's greatest twentieth-century president on the basis of his leadership throughout the Great Depression and World War II. Many view Churchill as Roosevelt's British equivalent. This psychocultural study contrasts these two leaders with Lincoln to help explain why our sixteenth president not only remains our best leader but holds the same position among all the world's democratic leaders.

This essay suggests that Lincoln's leadership ability was not unique. Other American presidents have exhibited similar "active-flexible" personalities. In fact, all four Mount Rushmore presidents share certain traits. Other political leaders have possessed essentially the same kind of temperament. They too were self-actualized through the political arena, deriving their greatest satisfaction from working on public policy issues.

I conclude this collection with an essay I wrote with Mark E. Neely Jr. about collecting artifacts, my original path to Lincoln at a young age. There are a finite number of Lincoln artifacts dating to his own time, but interest continues in other forms: tributes in sculpture, paintings, stamps, journals, books, et cetera. As Lincoln is embedded in the American political culture and is becoming increasingly so in the international culture of democracy, these artifacts have skyrocketed in price. Yet that has not destroyed or diminished Lincoln's legacy. Research since 1945 has dispelled the myth of Lincoln the saint, and the amateur collector has been priced out of the market, but Lincoln's ideas endure.

I look forward to the bicentennial of Lincoln's birth in 2009. The post–World War II generations have balanced the deified Lincoln by restoring his human dimension. Equally important, they have validated his contributions to the nation and begun to share this information to a greater extent than ever before. My hope is that the essays in this collection contribute, however modestly, to this effort.

Judging Lincoln

1

Abraham Lincoln,
Our Ever-Present Contemporary

AMERICANS ARE ambivalent about authority figures and heroes. Our revolutionary past makes us skeptics — at least it turned us against monarchs if not presidents. Our typical experience with political leaders tends to confirm our suspicions. Nonetheless, modern political science suggests the public's close identification with presidents.[1] Assassination and death in office undermine our skepticism, and after losing presidents we tend to overcompensate and turn them into saints. Yet George Washington and Thomas Jefferson were beloved. Neither was assassinated or died in office. Over time, however, we fall back on traditional doubts and wear presidents down while in office, then turn them into saints in death, only to tear them down again later. In part this sinner-saint cycle is a way for citizens to identify with the American political tradition that is reflected in the chief executive. In his book *Cincinnatus,* Garry Wills has aptly caught the saintly side of this process in the death of George Washington, and I will explore the cycle more fully in the life and death of our first assassinated president, Abraham Lincoln, whom scholars unanimously and consistently select as America's greatest president.

Lincoln in Power: Sinner to Sainthood

The names and labels given Lincoln in his lifetime reflect how he was treated as a politician. Abuse was hurled freely from the North during his first year as president. His supposed inadequacy and vacillation were condemned widely,

Reprinted with permission of the publisher from *"We Cannot Escape History": Lincoln and the Last Best Hope of Earth,* ed. James M. McPherson (Urbana: University of Illinois Press, 1995). © 1995 University of Illinois Press. This essay, presented with 140 slide illustrations in an earlier version at the Huntington Library conference on October 15, 1993, was based on my years of writing an annual Lincolniana article for the *Journal of the Abraham Lincoln Association,* the *Lincoln Herald,* and *Lincoln Lore.* I am indebted to William D. Pederson of Louisiana State University for his indispensable editorial assistance.

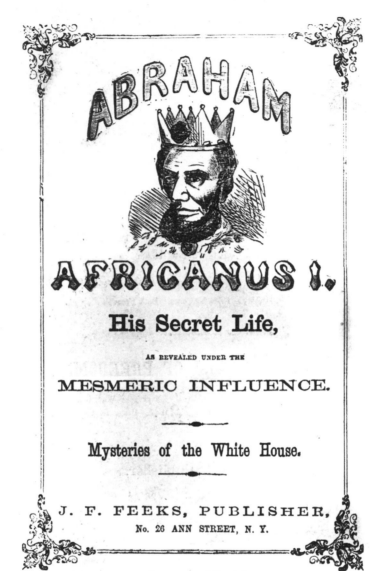

along with his intellect: "You cannot . . . fill his . . . empty skull with brains." He was a "political coward," "timid and ignorant," "pitiable," "too slow," "two faced," a man of "no education, shattered, dazed, utterly foolish," "an awful, woeful ass," a "blackguard," the "craftiest and most dishonest politician that ever disgraced an office in America," a "filthy story-teller," a "half-witted usurper," the "head ghoul at Washington," "a mold-eyed monster with a soul of leather," "Abraham Africanas I," an "obscene clown," an "orangutan," the "present turtle at the head of government, a slang-wanging, stump speaker," an "unmentionable disease," and the "wooden head at Washington."[2] At the very least the press saw Lincoln as ambiguous: Some newspapers supported him for being a Radical liberal and some for being a conservative. Thus he was criticized regardless of his actual position.

The attacks continued during the Civil War and of course were even harsher in the rebellious South. Even his cabinet consisted of fellow politicians who initially shared many of these views. In a sense, the general public caught on to the Lincoln message before much elite opinion did. As David E. Long argues in his exhaustive analysis of the 1864 election, the public's reaction to Lincoln's leadership even surprised the president, who was certain of his electoral defeat although equally convinced of the soundness of his policies.

Lincoln became part of the national myth before the assassination, when most people think the myth began. The letters to the president that are part of the Robert Todd Lincoln Collection in the Library of Congress show a clear progression in how Lincoln was viewed before and after he signed the preliminary Emancipation Proclamation in September 1862. After issuing the preliminary proclamation, he was regarded as more than a mere statesman. Of course, his assassination ensured the transformation of the reelected president from a politician into a saint who would certainly challenge, if not surpass, George Washington's apotheosis.

Lincoln knew how to write poetic prose. At his First Inaugural, he said, "We are not enemies, but friends. . . . Though passion may have strained, it must not break our bonds of affection. The mystic chords of memory, stretching from every battle-field, and patriot grave, to every living heart and hearthstone, all over this broad land, will yet swell the chorus of the Union, when again touched, as surely they will be, by the better angels of our nature."[3]

D. B. Russell, *Proclamation of Emancipation*. Boston, 1865. Broadside, 24 × 20 inches. Most modern Americans realize that Lincoln's signing of the Emancipation Proclamation was the act of a great statesman and not merely that of a politician or commander in chief. Bibliographer Charles Eberstadt has identified fifty-two emancipation broadsides attesting to the importance of and public appreciation for the president's proclamation. From The Frank and Virginia Williams Collection of Lincolniana; photograph by Claire White-Peterson, Mystic Seaport Museum.

Entered, according to Act of Congress in the year 1865, by J. A. Arthur, in the Clerk's Office of the District Court for the Eastern District of Pennsylvania.
WASHINGTON & LINCOLN: (APOTHEOSIS.)
S. J. Ferris, Pinxt.   Photo. and Pub. by Phil. Pho. Co., 730 Chestnut St.

S. J. Ferris, *Washington and Lincoln: (Apotheosis)*. Pennsylvania, 1865. *Carte-de-visite* photograph 4 × 2½ inches. After Lincoln's death, many artists and photographers created imagined scenes depicting Abraham Lincoln as a saint being received in heaven by the first president. From The Frank and Virginia Williams Collection of Lincolniana; photograph by Virginia Williams.

Although peace seemed imminent, Lincoln devoted fully half of his Second Inaugural Address to a fire-and-brimstone defense of the war as punishment sent from Heaven for the sin of slavery. He called it "strange" that both sides invoked God's "aid against the other," with "the prayers of neither . . . answered fully." Although convinced that the speech would "wear as well as — perhaps better than — anything" he had ever written, he was also aware that it was "not immediately popular," explaining, "Men are not flattered by being shown that there has been a difference of purpose between the almighty and them."[4]

But to Gary Lamolinara, the Second Inaugural is "probably the most famous of all inaugural addresses. . . . The power of its sentiment is deepened even further when it is read as a counterpoint to the first Inaugural Address, perhaps as Lincoln meant it to be. . . . On both occasions, he cited the responsibilities of the opposing sections, North and South, as well as his own as Chief Magistrate. . . . Lincoln . . . both times appealed to the basic humanity of the nation's citizenry, hoping that 'the mystic chords of memory' would 'swell the chorus of the Union' and lead to that transcendent moment when all could say, 'With malice toward none, with charity for all.'"[5]

Most people argue that the Gettysburg Address is not only his best work but also the most eloquent statement of the American political dream. The historian James A. Stevenson has suggested that Lincoln's life might have inspired the character of Huck Finn. The parallels to Lincoln's life found in this greatest of American novels are striking.

Presidential Usage: Hero and Justification

If writers were inspired and influenced by Abraham Lincoln, subsequent presidents have been, too. Unfortunately, few subsequent presidents have truly understood Lincoln's leadership, although nearly all have tried to "get right with Lincoln," as David Herbert Donald has aptly described the process. According to Donald, Lincoln's "ambiguity" has satisfied every conceivable national and political need, even for those who hold diametrically opposed views.[6]

Theodore Roosevelt, for example, was inspired by Lincoln and identified with his life. His "stewardship theory" of presidential power was an extreme version of Lincoln's wartime presidency. Alan Brinkley believes, "Great Presidents are products not just of their own talents and ambitions, but of the circumstances they inherit. Theodore Roosevelt complained frequently that his times had denied him greatness. 'A man has to take advantage of his opportunities,' he said after leaving office, 'but the opportunities have to come. If there is not the war, you don't get the great general; if there is not the great occasion, you don't get the great statesman; if Lincoln had lived in times of peace, no one would know his name now.'" Despite his successful activist presidency, Roosevelt was greatly disappointed that World War I came after he had left office, believing ruefully that Woodrow Wilson and not he had been given the opportunity for greatness.

C. Northcote Parkinson observed that "work expands so as to fill the time available for its completion."[7] Efforts of other presidents to wear Lincoln's mantle expanded, like Parkinson's law, to fill the time available for its use. Mired in the Great Depression, Herbert Hoover took solace in remembering that Lincoln had survived much abuse and was still reelected.[8]

Franklin Delano Roosevelt, not satisfied to claim Jefferson and Jackson, wanted to appropriate Abraham Lincoln for the Democratic Party in an effort to win votes, particularly those of African Americans.[9] Roosevelt invoked Lincoln's name at every possible opportunity, placing himself in a direct line of political descent from the martyred rail-splitter. During the presidential campaign of 1948, Harry Truman asserted that a twentieth-century Lincoln would clearly have been a regular Democrat.[10]

In delivering his farewell to the people of Massachusetts, President-elect John F. Kennedy consciously imitated Lincoln's Farewell Address to his friends in Springfield and did not object when his civil rights bill was termed the Second Emancipation Proclamation. Lyndon B. Johnson compared his Vietnam War ordeal to that of Abraham Lincoln, as did Richard M. Nixon, who visited the Lincoln Memorial late at night during Watergate to commune with his predecessor.[11]

During the 1992 presidential race, Lincoln seemed to belong to both Bill Clinton and George Bush. According to Eleanor Clift, at the time of the Gennifer Flowers revelation, Clinton was seen publicly leafing through the books *Lincoln on Democracy* and *Lincoln on Leadership,* and Bush compared himself to Lincoln, "a lonely White House occupant." Perhaps because the president is a symbol of national unity and stability, Lincoln is used shamelessly for political ends: Clinton has quoted Lincoln to justify activist government.

Many encouraged Bush to dump Dan Quayle as his vice presidential running mate, citing Lincoln's replacement of Hannibal Hamlin. William F. Buckley Jr. advised voters not to ignore Bush just "because he is not Abraham Lincoln."[12]

And then there was the case of former president Ronald Reagan, who brought a reverential silence to the 1992 Republican National Convention by invoking "Lincoln's words": "You cannot strengthen the weak by weakening the strong. You cannot help the wage-earner by pulling down the wage-payer. You cannot help the poor by destroying the rich. You cannot help men permanently by doing for them what they could and should do for themselves." The problem was, however, that these words were written not by Lincoln but by a former clergyman from Erie, Pennsylvania, in 1916. They were used from time to time during the 1930s by anti–New Deal businessmen and in 1942 by the right-wing Committee for Constitutional Government. Then, in 1950, Representative Frances Bolton of Ohio read them into the *Congressional Record* as Lincoln's maxims, and *Look* magazine gave them a full-page spread. "There seems to be no way," a Library of Congress report observed in May 1950, "of stopping the proliferation of the mistaken attribution."[13]

To Robert Hughes, the Australian art critic of *Time* magazine, "If the collective work that is America . . . is broken, the possibilities of Americanness begin to unravel. If they are fraying now, it is because the politics of ideology has, for the last twenty years, weakened, and, in some areas, broken the traditional American genius for consensus." Hughes maintains that "Reagan educated America down to his level. He left his country a little stupider in 1988 than it had been in 1980, and a lot more tolerant of lies." It did not matter, argues Hughes, that Reagan misquoted Lincoln. "Who was counting? For Reagan's fans, the idea that there ought to be . . . some relationship between utterance and source seemed impertinent to the memory of his presidency. This was not . . . Presidential character that Lincoln . . . [could] imagine—or respect."[14] Reagan was drawn to the Lincoln he envisioned and, as a result, did not portray him accurately. The press, with its own picture of Lincoln, was quick to expose the misrepresentation.[15]

Thirty years after John F. Kennedy's farewell remarks were compared to Lincoln's, Bill Clinton left for Washington with yet another Lincolnesque (or at least Lincoln-inspired) farewell. Upon leaving Springfield, Lincoln said:

> My friends—No one, not in my situation, can appreciate my feeling of sadness at this parting. To this place, and the kindness of these people, I

owe every thing. . . . I now leave, not knowing when, or whether ever, I may return, with a task before me greater than that which rested upon Washington. Without the assistance of that Divine Being, . . . I cannot succeed. With that assistance I cannot fail. . . . Let us confidently hope that all will yet be well. To His care commending you, as I hope in your prayers you will commend me, I bid you an affectionate farewell.[16]

Upon leaving Little Rock, Clinton said:

I'll miss my whole network of friends and what I can do. I'll miss going down to the Y in the morning, my blue-collar gym, where there's nobody in bright Spandex outfits. I have a lot of friends in Washington. I think I'll enjoy it a lot.[17]

Of course, Lincoln sounds better than Clinton, but Harold Holzer has observed that much of Lincoln's reputation as an orator—especially in the Lincoln-Douglas debates—was a myth. Has the nation's view of leadership and the presidency changed? George Bush was never able to overcome the reversal of his 1988 pledge of no new taxes. When he did support additional taxes, he "invoked" the words of Lincoln, explaining, "I'm doing like Lincoln did, 'think anew,'" quoting from the president's annual message to Congress on December 1, 1862, in which Lincoln called not only for restoration of the Union but also for freeing the slaves—albeit gradually. During his 1860 campaign, Lincoln had vowed that the federal government should not interfere with slavery where it existed.[18]

Americans reelected Lincoln; they were less charitable to Bush in 1992. Still, Lincoln's contemporaries did not universally recognize his greatness. As time passes, citizens perceive and evaluate presidents in terms of their stands on issues, party connections, leadership, and personal qualities.[19] Time and reflection have been kinder to Abraham Lincoln than to most presidents, despite their real and contrived identification with him.

Perhaps we should not be too harsh on presidential reliance on Lincoln, for his successors merely try to come to terms with the man who has set the standard for presidential leadership and perhaps democratic leadership in general. Lincoln satisfies every international need: Lincoln the nationalist (for the early-nineteenth-century Italians trying to form a nation), Lincoln the democrat (for the early-nineteenth-century French), and Lincoln the libertarian (for his few English admirers at the time of his presidency). From this worldview it is possible to understand how a young Chinese boy learned about Abraham Lincoln at a school in Honolulu and then remembered the Gettysburg Address when he returned home. Sun Yat-sen went on to become the first president of modern China and turned to the declaration when formulating his political creed, *San min chu-yi* (three people's principles), which correspond with "of the people [*Min you*], by the people [*Min chih*], and for the people [*Min hsiang*]."[20]

Richard N. Current has reported that when he was in India in 1959 on the occasion of the Lincoln sesquicentennial, people made constant comparison between Lincoln and Gandhi, almost always to Gandhi's advantage (although a Lion's Club member in Patna assured Current that there would have been no partition of Pakistan from India had Lincoln been in charge).

There is plenty of Lincoln to go around. He is in Poland, too, thanks to Mario M. Cuomo's publication, in Polish, of a Lincoln anthology about liberty and democracy.[21] When the Baltic states seceded from the Soviet Union, some thought that doing so was contrary to the principles of the Union that Lincoln espoused. Eric Foner, a Fulbright professor at Moscow University in 1990, has observed that Lincoln, like Gorbachev, would have opposed the independence of the Baltic states, the implication being that the United States was inconsistent in opposing Confederate independence in 1861 and favoring Baltic independence in 1990. However, there is a great difference between the United States in 1861 and the Soviet Union in 1991. Jonathan Schell opines, "If the Union means the willing consent of people to forge a common destiny, the Soviet Union died long ago. Its government no longer represented a majority anywhere." To put it in terms of the United States in 1861, it would have been as if "*all* of the states had sought to secede." This is no contradiction, because Gorbachev's role was to preside over dissolving a Union, whereas Lincoln is rightly honored for saving one.

Pop Culture and Lincoln

If subsequent presidents have found it difficult to meet Lincoln's performance standard, the general public must contend with the Lincoln standard enshrined in the Lincoln Memorial and on Mount Rushmore. Like ordinary presidents, ordinary mortals find it difficult to grapple with saintly stature and reduce it to their level. Even if doing so diminishes the heroic, it at least shows the struggle that later generations experience in coming to terms with quality.

The contrast is found, for example, in Gutzon Borglum's statue of Lincoln in Newark, New Jersey. Lincoln is shown seated on a bench, which allows the public to share space and thoughts with him. The work is clearly a tribute to Lincoln, and it captures his spirit. In contrast, the J. Seward Johnson Jr. statue unveiled in Gettysburg in November 1991 portrays Lincoln with an anonymous modern figure. The public is excluded from interacting with the piece. Its intent is commercial, an effort to sell Gettysburg tourism. This is not a tribute to Lincoln but an appropriation of his good name.

The emphasis on Lincoln's rise from poverty, the journey from log cabin to White House, has been superseded by a fragmented view of a sick man who suffered from depression and Marfan's Syndrome. The National Museum of Health and Science has recommended testing a sample of Lincoln's blood to determine his DNA, prompting one commentator to ask, "Can Abraham Lincoln's DNA be cloned? . . . not to diagnose his diseases, but to fill today's leadership gap."[22] The museum tabled the issue until, it said, testing is perfected, but perhaps it also feared being made the butt of jokes. Too late. The *Weekly World News,* a tabloid, reported on October 5, 1993, that doctors at Walter Reed Army Medical Hospital had exhumed Lincoln's body, immersed it in a "special solution," and then injected a "resurrection drug." Lincoln was said to have been revived for ninety-five seconds, time enough to ask, "Gentlemen, where am I?"[23]

Yet Philip B. Kunhardt Jr. and Philip B. Kunhardt III's ABC miniseries *Lincoln,* Ken Burns's PBS series *The Civil War,* and David Grubin's miniseries *Abraham and Mary Lincoln: A House Divided* are, according to Harry F. Waters writing in *Newsweek,* all part of television's "latest programming twist: the history lesson. Documentary makers and their corporate patrons are simultaneously feeding and exploiting a burgeoning appetite for the stuff of America's past." Traditionally, history draws big audiences on a regular basis.

The television view of Lincoln reaches millions. But what view? Documentaries aside, with all of the great Lincoln plays available for production and televising, all the viewing audience saw on April 21, 1991, was Dennis Brown's ABC movie *A Perfect Tribute,* which centered more on the story of a young boy who leaves home to find his Confederate brother than on President Lincoln.

The avoidance of Lincoln's racial views in the Kunhardts' production of *Lincoln* in December 1992 also contributes to this reworking and perhaps represents a social statement about the nation's reluctance to face racism. Forty percent of the documentary was devoted to the assassination, demonstrating the enormous fascination that people still have with Lincoln's death, an interest to which the authors and producers evidently felt compelled to pander. Consider, for example, the popularity and large membership of the Surratt Society, a group dedicated to remembering fondly the woman who, at the very least, housed the assassination conspirators. Some argue that this phenomenon is similar to those who hallucinate over the Kennedy assassination or discover Elvis at the laundromat.

How we think about Lincoln tells us much about our culture. Anyone impersonating Napoleon is assumed to be slightly mad. Yet the Association of Lincoln Impersonators has more than one hundred card-carrying, accurately costumed Lincoln portrayers and a newsletter, *Lincarnations.* The Friends of the Presidential Entourage of Abraham Lincoln produce their own quarterly newsletter, *The Reviewing Stand.* People want to be entertained if they cannot fully understand; in either case, Lincoln makes people feel good. With so much culture shock from Lincoln being recast in the modern image, can we do no better than a Lincoln impersonator rolling down the highway in a Winnebago that looks like a log cabin? Each generation makes its own Lincoln, and he may not be the Lincoln known before.

The 1960s brought Disney's animated Lincoln. "Fantasy has been entirely abandoned," said Walt Disney of his then immensely popular life-size, automated Lincoln, which first performed in the Illinois pavilion at the 1964 New York World's Fair. For Disney, the homage was no gimmick but a new art form, "audio-animatronics," which, he believed, would "combine the best of traditional media to capture the real countenance, the warm sincerity, and the contagious dedication of Abraham Lincoln." Yet even Disney's Lincoln suffered from revision.[24] In 1990, Disneyland's officials planned to close "Great Moments with Mr. Lincoln" and replace him with Kermit the Frog. Tourists and park employees rebelled. As one boy said, "Lincoln was President. Kermit is a frog."[25] As with historians, Lincoln remains at the top of the popular culture polls. In a Disneyland election, he defeated Kermit.[26]

Nor is Lincoln ignored in literary and dramatic humor. In his one-act play *The Query,* Woody Allen presents a Lincoln who uses his press secretary as a straight man, getting him to ask at a press conference, "Mr. President, how long do you think a man's legs should be?" Lincoln responds, "Long enough to reach the ground." Caught up in the laughter, he ignores a distraught father seeking a pardon for his son. And the bane of academicians is that people everywhere wonder what Lincoln would do if he were alive today. In 1984, James M. McPherson appeared on a radio station in Wilmington after speaking to the Lincoln Group of Delaware. The first question he was asked was, "If Lincoln were alive today, what position would he take on abortion and the budget deficit?"[27]

Minority Groups: Emancipator, Oppressor, and Equal

In some ways the most interesting use of Lincoln has been made by emerging social and political groups: African Americans, the women's movement, the men's movement, and the gay pride movement, for example. This is clearest in the long African American struggle to achieve equality. For example, the records of the Federal Writers Project in Washington, D.C., contain a recollection by a former slave, Fanny Burdock of Valdosta, Georgia, who was born in the 1840s:

> We been picking in the field when my brother he point to the road and then we seen Marse Abe coming all dusty on foot. We run right to the fence and had the oak bucket and dipper. When he draw up to us, he so tall, black eyes so sad. Didn't say not one word, just looked hard at all us, every one us crying. We give him nice cool water from the dipper. Then he nodded and set off and we just stood there till he get to being dust then nothing. After, didn't our owner or nobody credit it, but me and all my kin, we knowed. I still got the dipper to prove it.

Allan Gurganus's novel *The Oldest Living Confederate Widow Tells All* begins with that very recollection and then points out, "In reality, Lincoln's foot tour of Georgia could not have happened. In this book, it can. Such scenes were told by hundreds of slaves. Such visitations remain, for me, truer than fact. History is my starting point."[28]

The African American perception of Lincoln remains varied and ambiguous. Joseph Fowlkes, past president of the Providence chapter of the NAACP, has said that the Emancipation Proclamation "was almost bogus, a lot of sound and fury, but there was no real enforcement power behind it."[29] He obviously had not read the results of Mark Neely's research in the

National Archives, which reveals that Union commanders in the field dealt harshly with slave owners, including long prison sentences for those who failed to obey or recognize the proclamation. And John Hope Franklin calls the proclamation "momentous," adding, "There was no chance slavery could survive after that." Barbara Fields contends the slaves emancipated themselves, further contributing to the reworking of Lincoln's image as the Great Emancipator. Another attempt to answer the question of who freed the slaves comes from McPherson, who credits Lincoln, primarily because he would have war rather than allow secession. And without Civil War there would have been "no confiscation act, no Emancipation Proclamation, no Thirteenth Amendment, certainly no self-emancipation and almost certainly no end of slavery for several more decades."[30]

Lincoln's contemporary ups and downs with the black community began in the 1960s when *Ebony* published "Was Abe Lincoln a White Supremacist?" by Lerone Bennett Jr., and they continue with Bennett's 2000 book, *Forced into Glory: Abraham Lincoln's White Dream*. Bennett asserted that Lincoln was a racist, citing doubtful evidence and using selectivity and more than some misrepresentation. Conceding that historians can judge the past, one can still doubt the fairness of a verdict based entirely on ex post facto standards.[31]

The ultimate irony may be that in the African American struggle to achieve equality Lincoln has been democratized to the point that his presidency has been reduced to failure such as Warren Harding's, with the recent advent of Presidents' Day replacing the observation of the birthdays of George Washington and Abraham Lincoln.

In the October 1992 issue of *American Heritage Magazine,* Daniel Aaron explored whether any historical novel may be true history. In a continuation of his decades-long thrust against Lincoln "scholar squirrels," Gore Vidal also argues that the past cannot be left to "hagiographers" whose perspective is too narrow to grasp the mind of Lincoln fully. He contends that his *Lincoln: A Novel* (1984) is grounded in historical sources. Yet historians have accused Vidal of gross distortions and inaccuracies in his depiction of Lincoln as "coarse-grained and devious, ignorant of economics, disregardful of the Constitution, fiercely ambitious, and a racist until the end." Vidal also has been said to have relied on outdated and discredited bits of scholarship and oversimplified complex issues. Although agreeing that he "embellished here and there," Vidal has insisted that he used primary sources. He has pointed out in *Screening History* that Americans prefer films based upon romanticized episodes from the lives of such European royalty as Henry VIII, Elizabeth I, or Napoleon but have no interest in Lincoln's presidency.

The gay issue is not to be ignored, either. Consider Robert Bly's discussion of whether gays should be allowed in the military. Among the highland Mayans in Guatemala, Bly found, knowledge is presented in four stages for men: the boy, the warrior, the community man, and the "echo" man. The step from boy to warrior is fundamental, and although he is admired, the young warrior is still not considered a finished male. The community man lives for the community, taking care of widows and orphans and using his earlier developed warrior disciplines to protect them. The last stage, the "echo" man, is a person who hears; he is all ears, all grief, all intuition, and all responsive to sound. The Gettysburg Address is the speech of a true "echo" man. In speaking of a debt to forefathers and to the living and to the soldiers who have just died, he hears grief. In "What the Mayans Could Teach the Joint Chiefs," Bly attempts to mitigate the military's fears of gays: "We justly admire and value the warrior, but we need not act on all of his fears. Having a wider vision, we can bless the warriors and keep the sad and echoing face of Lincoln before us."[32]

Conclusion

A review of the sinner-saint cycle suggests why Abraham Lincoln remains an everlasting contemporary. His performance in the White House set the standard of presidential and democratic leadership. If subsequent presidents, pop culture, and minority groups have a difficult time contending with a myth, their abuse and misuse of the Lincoln standard should not be judged too harshly. After all, historians have also created idealized versions of Lincoln in prose and poetry as well as revisionist accounts.[33]

Of course, Abraham Lincoln began the cycle himself. He was a common person who became uncommon, a Machiavellian politician who became a statesman. His leadership style is one of America's greatest gifts to democracy. Preservation of the Union grew into a democratic justification for self-government's emphasis on dignity and equality as necessary for self-realization. He matured as a political leader, fulfilling himself in the public eye and extending the democratic burden to everyone, a contemporary and the personification of "the last best, hope of earth."[34]

Notes

1. Greenstein, 121.

2. Randall, "Vindictives and Vindication."

3. *Collected Works of Abraham Lincoln,* 4:271.

4. Cuomo and Holzer, "Lincoln's Second Inaugural Address."

5. Lamolinara, 33.

6. Donald, "Getting Right with Lincoln," 18.

7. Stevenson, "Parkinson, Eighty-three, Dies."

8. Fehrenbacher, *The Changing Image,* 3–4.

9. Kammen, 48; Abbott.

10. Fehrenbacher, *The Changing Image,* 3.

11. Ibid.

12. Willing; Tullai, "The Precedent for Dumping a V.P."; Buckley.

13. Schlesinger, "The History of Those Words Lincoln Never Said."

14. Hughes, 43.

15. Mitgang, "Reagan's 'Lincoln' Quotation Disputed."

16. *Collected Works,* 4:190–91.

17. *Illinois Times,* January 21, 1993.

18. See Tullai, "Mr. Bush Tries Out Abe-Speak."

19. Greenstein, 141.

20. Mitgang, "Abraham Lincoln: Friend of a Free Press," 106.

21. Cuomo and Holzer, eds., *Lincoln on Democracy.*

22. Lowenstein.

23. Dexter.

24. Henderson.

25. Greenstein, 129.

26. Williams, "Lincolniana in 1991."

27. J. McPherson, preface to *Abraham Lincoln and the Second American Revolution,* ix.

28. Gurganus, xvi.

29. Quoted in "Emancipation Proclamation Draws Large Crowds in D.C.," *Providence Journal-Bulletin,* January 5, 1993.

30. Neely, "Lincoln and the Theory of Self-Emancipation"; Franklin; Fields; J. McPherson, *Who Freed the Slaves?,* 3.

31. Fehrenbacher, *The Changing Image,* 23.

32. See also William V. Davis.

33. Tarbell, *The Early Life of Abraham Lincoln;* Sandburg.

34. *Collected Works,* 5:537.

2

"A Matter of Profound Wonder": The Women in Lincoln's Life

FIRST LET ME STATE what this paper is not. It is not a series of biographical sketches about the women in Lincoln's life, nor is it a treatise on
whether he was referring to his natural mother or his stepmother when he
called one of them "my angel mother."[1] And it does not examine whether it
is, as Lincoln himself put it, "a matter of profound wonder"[2] that he finally
married Mary Todd.

But I do hope to suggest an interpretation of the personality of Abraham
Lincoln through relationships he had with women and how that influenced
his style of leadership. Although some of the relationships are sparsely documented, a pattern emerges that strongly suggests the development of a nor-
mal, healthy personality. The record shows he valued women as individuals,
treated them with respect and equality, and learned from them. He would
apply these traits in his public policies. Lincoln advocated a major advancement in equality because women had taught him the values of human dignity.

Early Bonding with Women

The first three women in Lincoln's life were his mother, Nancy Hanks Lincoln, his stepmother, Sarah Bush Johnston Lincoln, and his sister Sarah Lincoln. Although the information is limited, the picture is clear. He valued his
mothers as "angels." When he lost his mother, he was deeply shaken, a loss

Reprinted with permission of the publisher from the *Papers of the Eleventh and Twelfth Annual Lincoln Colloquium of the Lincoln Home,* ed. Linda Norbut Suits and Timothy P. Townsend (Springfield, Ill.: Lincoln
Home National Historic Site), and was originally delivered at the Twelfth Annual Lincoln Colloquium at
the Lincoln Home National Historic Site in Springfield on October 25, 1997. © 1997 Lincoln Home
National Historic Site. I thank William D. Pederson and Harold Holzer for their close reading and suggestions. A special thanks to my law clerk, Erika Leigh Kruse, for her editorial assistance and for ensur-
ing that I correctly portrayed Lincoln's feminine qualities.

Mrs. Lincoln.

Entered according to the act of Congress, in the year 1861, by M B. BRADY, in the Clerk's office of the District Court of the District of Columbia.

Mathew B. Brady, [Mary Lincoln]. New York, 1861. *Carte-de-visite* photograph, 4 × 2½ inches. This full-length standing pose of Mrs. Lincoln was widely distributed by the Brady Gallery and—judging by the number of surviving copies—was very popular with the public. From The Frank and Virginia Williams Collection of Lincolniana; photograph by Virginia Williams.

perhaps triggering later episodes of depression. And it is also clear that he maintained his relationship with his stepmother, showing concern for her welfare.

Though very little is known about his sister, her early death seems to have contributed further to his tendency to melancholy. In each of these relationships, Lincoln emerges as a deeply caring man, able to empathize with others who lost loved ones. We see this in the letter he wrote in the 1860s, with the nation embroiled in civil war, to young Fanny McCullough, the daughter of an old Illinois friend who died in battle.

Dear Fanny

It is with deep grief that I learn of the death of your kind and brave Father; and, especially, that it is affecting your young heart beyond what is common in such cases. In this sad world of ours, sorrow comes to all; and, to the young, it comes with bitterest agony, because it takes them unawares. The older have learned to ever expect it. I am anxious to afford some alleviation of your present distress. Perfect relief is not possible, except with time. You can not now realize that you will ever feel better. Is not this so? And yet it is a mistake. You are sure to be happy again. To know this, which is certainly true, will make you some less miserable now. I have had experience enough to know what I say; and you need only to believe it, to feel better at once. The memory of your dear Father, instead of an agony, will yet be a sad sweet feeling in your heart, of a purer, and holier sort than you have known before. Please present my kind regards to your afflicted mother.

Your sincere friend,

A. Lincoln[3]

His letters to Fanny McCullough as well as to Mrs. Bixby, who, the president believed, lost five sons in the Civil War, emanate compassion and empathy: "I feel how weak and fruitless must be any words of mine which should attempt to beguile you from the grief of a loss so overwhelming."[4] Lincoln emerges as profound and sensitive, expressing his empathy and tenderness, despite the demands of war on the president.

Executive Mansion
May 21. 1862.

Hon. Senator Simmons
    My dear Sir:
        This distressed
girl says she belongs to your
state; that she was here with
her father and brother, in
our Army, till they went
with it to the peninsula; that
her has been killed there, &
his father made prisoner —
and that she is here,
wanting employment to support herself — If you can be
satisfied that her story is
correct, please see if you
can not get Mr. Sec. Chase
or friend Newton to find her
a place. Yours truly A. Lincoln

Abraham Lincoln, autographed letter. Washington, D.C., May 21, 1862, to Senator James F. Simmons of Rhode Island. The president's concern about a "distressed girl" demonstrates his sensitivity as well as his ability to write succinctly. It also suggests a compassion and empathy toward women. From The Frank and Virginia Williams Collection of Lincolniana; photograph by Claire White-Peterson, Mystic Seaport Museum.

Searching for a Significant Other

Between his leaving home and his eventual marriage, Lincoln sought the company of women. The pattern in this stage of his life seems to range from tragedy to humor. His short relationship with Ann Rutledge may have been his first true love, but unfortunately it ended tragically. Yet the mere existence of this relationship suggests a Lincoln searching for a significant other. His subsequent awkward and bumbling relationship with Mary Owens imparts the same motivation. He was still searching. Married women who knew him also showed their concern by trying to find him a wife.

Photographer unknown, *Mrs. Lincoln* (on reverse) (detail). Undated. *Carte-de-visite* photograph, 4 × 2½ inches. This photograph is not included in *The Photographs of Mary Todd Lincoln* by Lloyd Ostendorf (*Journal of the Illinois State Historical Society,* 1969). Mary Todd Lincoln was the most important woman in Lincoln's life. From The Frank and Virginia Williams Collection of Lincolniana; photograph by Virginia Williams.

John Adams Whipple, the Lincoln home, Springfield (detail). Published by
Charles Desilver, Philadelphia, 1860. Photograph, 5⅞ × 7⅞ inches. Lincoln is
shown with his sons Willie and Tad in front of his Springfield, Illinois, residence, the only home he ever owned. The indistinct figure in front of the wall
is Isaac Diller, a playmate of the Lincoln boys. He moved as the photograph was
being taken, and only his boots and the stripes on his socks were captured in
the picture. From The Frank and Virginia Williams Collection of Lincolniana;
photograph by Virginia Williams.

Marriage and Maturity: Equality

The best-documented woman in Lincoln's life is Mary Todd. His motivation to marry is clear. He married up, and she polished him as much as she could. Mary, too, was an "engine that knew no rest"[5] in promoting and encouraging his political advancement. Theirs may have been a turbulent marriage, but they learned to deal with one another's deficits to forge an enduring relationship that was enriched by the love they had for their children. Less well documented is how Lincoln treated his wife and Mariah Vance, their Springfield housekeeper. The picture that emerges is that he treated women, whether a well-born Southern belle or a lowly African American laundress (and her family),[6] with respect, concern, and even affection. The Emancipation Proclamation was not an aberration in Lincoln's life, nor was his willingness to support women's rights.

Photographer unknown, the Lincoln home. Springfield, Illinois, 1865. Photograph, 6 × 8¾ inches. Dorothy Meserve Kunhardt and Philip B. Kunhardt Jr., in their *Twenty Days*, identified this photograph as showing members of the official congressional committee that accompanied Lincoln's remains to Springfield, arriving on May 3, 1865. The man on the left, inside the fence, is Congressman Isaac N. Arnold of Illinois, to whom Mrs. Lincoln would tell the story of her husband's request to be laid "in some quiet place." From The Frank and Virginia Williams Collection of Lincolniana; photograph by Claire White-Peterson, Mystic Seaport Museum.

Leadership: Masculine or Feminine

Lincoln exemplifies democratic leadership and gives it an unexpected dimension. Contrary to the traditional association of leadership to masculinity and detached objectivity, the most haunting images of Lincoln often are unmistakably feminine.

"Lincoln is a man of heart—as gentle as a woman's and as tender," William Herndon said of his law partner, then president-elect.[7] Yet not all observers considered Lincoln's feminine qualities as an attribute. Historian Francis Parkman ranked Lincoln well below Washington as a president because Lincoln "failed to meet his standard that men should be masculine and women feminine."[8] But the more typical view of Lincoln was expressed by Robert Ingersoll, Republican politician and celebrated agnostic, in a line that evokes nineteenth-century sentimentality but is still touching: "He is the gentlest memory of our world."[9]

Yet Lincoln's tender heart was tempered by a staunch will and resolute disposition. After citing Lincoln's tender feelings, Herndon immediately emphasized that "he has a will strong as iron."[10] Charles Dana, Lincoln's assistant secretary of war, recalled that "one always felt the presence of a will and an intellectual power which maintained the ascendancy of the President."[11]

Lincoln's control of his temper and virility demanded considerable self-discipline. As a young man active in partisan politics, Lincoln had become embroiled in a number of personal contentions where his combative personality would surface. In 1842 he almost found himself in a duel with the Illinois state auditor, James Shields, who was outraged over a satirical attack that Lincoln had published under a pseudonym. Lincoln responded indignantly to a political handbill that distorted his own legislative record, vowing to the voters of Sangamon County, "All I have to say is that the author is a liar and a scoundrel, and that if he will avow the authorship to me, I promise to give his proboscis a good wringing."[12]

Lincoln displayed qualities that should have satisfied the most strident advocates of manliness in his flexible determination to carry the Civil War through to a successful conclusion, as in his sarcastic complaint about those who fought the war with "elder-stalk squirts, charged with rose water,"[13] and in his willingness to endorse such brutal methods of warfare as those used by William Tecumseh Sherman. Conventional definitions of masculinity were not foreign to his own thought and were apparent in his response to those who appealed to him to let the South secede: "There is no Washington in that—no Jackson in that—no manhood nor honor in that."[14]

Yet it can also be said that Lincoln's keen sense of timing and his ability to assess a difficult situation were based on the more feminine component of intuition.

Lincoln can thus be seen as a leader who was unusual in his ability to reconcile the masculine and feminine dimensions of his personality. Such a conclusion is a metaphorical statement about his character rather than a psychological statement about his sexual identity. Possessing and utilizing qualities that American culture has normally labeled as masculine and feminine, he had little in common with more exclusively masculine political leaders, such as Andrew Jackson and Ulysses S. Grant. Nonetheless, Lincoln's merging of his masculine/feminine traits was central to his practice of great leadership. In fact, the Lincoln example suggests that a great leader should synchronize the traditional masculine and feminine aspects of behavior. A leader should have the strength of purpose and tenacity of will that American culture has generally designated as masculine, as well as the sensitivity, openness, and willingness to nurture others, traits that American culture has typically viewed—and often disparaged—as women's ways.

Ethic of Care and Ethic of Rights

In order to understand Lincoln as a leader, it is necessary to look not only at his success in leading the nation but also at his dealings with individuals. He treated leadership as a *relationship* involving individuals as well as large groups. His compassionate and nurturing practices, his resistance to quarreling and his freedom from malice, most fully revealed his integrated masculine/feminine nature of leadership.

Without mentioning Lincoln by name, the work of Carol Gilligan shows how a person with Lincoln's character combines both masculine and feminine qualities. Gilligan suggests that the moral development of males usually entails the learning of an "ethic of rights" geared to "arriving at an objectively fair or just resolution to moral dilemmas." In contrast, women develop an "ethic of care" with its focus not on the application of abstract justice but on "sensitivity to the needs of others and consideration of other points of view." Lincoln has long been understood as one of America's greatest proponents of an "ethic of rights," for he is often quoted for his rigorous opposition to those who advocated the spread of slavery. However, Lincoln can also be understood as epitomizing an "ethic of care."[15]

Despite all the burdens and responsibilities of the Civil War presidency—major military strategy, recruitment of hundreds of thousands of troops, conflicts with Congress over emancipation and reconstruction—Lincoln insisted upon remaining accessible to individuals who wanted to see him personally. Although the time spent with all these visitors intensified Lincoln's exhaustion, he could not shut them out. He felt empathy with many of them. He told Senator Henry Wilson, "They don't want much; they get but little, and I must see them."[16] He described his hours spent with ordinary people in the White House as "public opinion baths."[17] He remained open to people and learned from them, just as he learned from the women in his life.

Of all the personal requests he received, Lincoln was most concerned with pleas for pardons. He did not always agree to grant pardons, and he ordered executions to be carried out in what he considered to be "very flagrant cases." Yet he granted so many pardons that stories of his clemency toward the condemned became a major part of his contemporary reputation and subsequent legend. The stories are largely true and genuinely moving and reveal not only a kind man but also a leader who knew political uses of kindness. As Richard Nelson Current observed, Lincoln

> had to deal with an army consisting mainly of citizen soldiers. . . . With such men as these, frequent pardons may have been bad for discipline, but the regimen of the regular army, if unrelieved, might have been even worse for morale. The service needed to be made as popular and attractive as it could be, and Lincoln's clemency made it less unattractive than it otherwise would have been.[18]

One does not, however, have to choose between an interpretation of Lincoln's pardons as saintly forgiveness or as canny politics, for Lincoln knew that what was kind was often political as well. This tenet he learned from the women in his life.

Lincoln's balanced temperament also allowed him to work with the Radicals amid storms of abuse. Lincoln opened himself fully to their arguments, meeting frequently with delegations, even attending antislavery lectures. And he was careful not to speak ill of the Radicals in public, no matter what they said publicly about him.

Executive Mansion,

Washington, May 5, 1864.

Gen. Benham.

Please suspend execution of privates Cusich and Gray. 15th N.Y. Eng's until further order.

A. Lincoln

Abraham Lincoln, autographed letter, Executive Mansion. Washington, D.C., May 5, 1864, to Brig. Gen. Henry Worthington Benham. Lincoln's compassionate recognition that most Union soldiers were volunteers inspired him to grant many pardons and suspend the execution of soldiers until he reviewed each individual record. Privates Cusich and Gray are not mentioned in *Don't Shoot That Boy! Abraham Lincoln and Military Justice* by Thomas P. Lowry. Nor was this letter included in *The Collected Works of Abraham Lincoln*. From The Frank and Virginia Williams Collection of Lincolniana; photograph by Claire White-Peterson, Mystic Seaport Museum.

The man who would avoid quarrels would also avoid resentment and grudges. Lincoln taught himself to resist antagonistic feelings toward those who had caused him grief. Having lost his mother as a child, Lincoln understood that anger was futile. The final passage of his Second Inaugural Address amplified a personal code of conduct expressed earlier in the war: "I shall do nothing in malice. What I deal with is too vast for malicious dealing."[19] Lincoln was outraged by the South's initial arguments for secession and assaults on free government, but he reminded himself to "judge not that we be not judged,"[20] and he planned to treat the miscreant section with magnanimity, if they would allow him. Although he was troubled by Secretary of the Treasury Chase's scheming to eliminate him for the 1864 Republican nomination, Lincoln treated Chase with patience and forgiveness, later nominating him as chief justice of the United States.

As Lincoln matured personally and politically, he began to construct the amiable and gentle self with whom we are familiar. In his eulogy for Zachary Taylor in 1850, there are several passages that reveal Lincoln's efforts to learn from Taylor a democratic leadership style free from contentiousness. Lincoln wrote of the former president, "He was alike averse to sudden, and to startling quarrels; and he pursued no man with revenge." Lincoln went on to praise Taylor's relationships with his troops: "Of the many who served with him through the long course of forty years, all testify to the uniform kindness, and his constant care for, and hearty sympathy with, their every want and every suffering; while none can be found to declare, that he was ever a tyrant anywhere, in anything."[21] These same words could be used to describe Lincoln as president.

Lincoln avoided quarrels and resentments not from a stance of superiority or indifference to his subordinates but from a genuine concern for the feelings of others. He did not treat subordinates as instruments of his masterful will but rather followed the dictates of an ethic of care and paid heed to their individual needs and feelings. For example, he wrote to Secretary of War Edwin Stanton that the change of command at New Orleans from General "X" to General "Y" "must be so managed as to not wrong, or wound the feelings of General Banks."[22]

This sincerity was rare in an American political leader but had been rooted in empathy and linked to the early women in his life. Having endured his share of wounded feelings, Lincoln wrote to James Hackett, "I have endured a great deal of ridicule without much malice; and have received a great deal of kindness, not quite free from ridicule."[23] But sensitivity was also an obligation for the kind of democratic leader that Lincoln sought to be. By avoiding quarrels, by shunning resentments, by paying attention to feelings, Lincoln could approach others with respect for their talents, their services, and their dignity, and thereby lessen the inherent distance between leader and subordinates. This sensitivity made possible a successful dialogue between leader and subordinates.

Lincoln's gentleness and kindness were not the marks of an effusive character. He could be aloof, brooding, and mysterious. But out of the depths of his multifaceted personality and in response to his experiences with women he developed a masculine/feminine temperament that governed his personal relationships. His fusion of an ethic of rights and an ethic of care was a matter of political conviction as well as personal nature.

LINCOLN   TAD   WILLIE   ROBERT   MRS. LINCOLN

LINCOLN AND FAMILY.

Printmaker unknown, *Lincoln and Family*. Undated. Lithograph, 18×23½ inches. Lincoln, shown here with *(from left to right)* Tad, Willie, Robert, and Mary, possessed both masculine and feminine qualities that made him a superb family man, yet the family was never photographed together. Prints like this one were composites. From The Frank and Virginia Williams Collection of Lincolniana; photograph by Virginia Williams.

As a democratic leader, Lincoln believed he must not only represent and educate the people collectively but also care for the dignity and needs of the individual.

Defending the humanity of the slave in the 1850s against the assaults of proslavery apologists, Lincoln had considered African Americans as passive victims of injustice. But during the Civil War he came to recognize African Americans as active and vital participants in the cause of democracy. He was particularly impressed by the contributions of African American soldiers. To detractors of the Emancipation Proclamation, he pointed out that when peace came and the Union was restored, "there will be some black men who can remember that, with silent tongue, and clenched teeth, and steady eye, and well-poised bayonet, they have helped mankind on to this great consummation; while, I fear, there will be some white ones, unable to forget that, with malignant heart, and deceitful speech, they have strove to hinder it."[24]

Democratic Purposes

Abraham Lincoln demonstrated how powerful ambition could be reconciled with — and serve — democratic purposes. He was history's most striking confirmation of John Adams's assertions about the political importance of the "passion for distinction." Lincoln had plenty of passion as well as being an advocate of reason, "cool, unimpassioned reason."

By moderating the masculine view of leadership, Lincoln achieved a masculine/feminine fusion that has been too little understood. He recognized that the democratic dignity of citizens requires nurture and that the democratic perspective of leaders requires an openness to the views of others and a sensitivity to their needs. His approach avoided paternalism — except perhaps in the case of African Americans about which he continued to learn, because he began from the premise of mutuality, always regarding ordinary citizens as capable of everything he himself had achieved. Lincoln's self-assertion was balanced with his regard for others. He overcame much of the distance between leaders and followers by identifying himself with those followers. In his final years, he demonstrated how democratic leadership could combine an abstract set of principles — an ethic of rights — with a concrete and empathetic ethic of care. Lincoln also demonstrated how an ethic of care could be practical politics. The side of him that is characterized as feminine neither undercut his masculine political skills nor weakened him as a leader.

William A. Patterson (1865–1939), after an 1860 photograph by Alexander Hesler, *Portrait of Abraham Lincoln.* Ca. 1930. Miniature portrait painted on ivory, 4¼×3½ inches. This is how Lincoln looked just weeks after his nomination for the presidency—still beardless, at last on the brink of national success and recognition. From The Frank and Virginia Williams Collection of Lincolniana; photograph by Virginia Williams.

Lincoln's career reveals the inadequacy of the hard-boiled perspective that equates leadership with power, dominance, and manipulation. He gained political support through his kindness and political insight through the mutuality of relationships. He was able to evolve into a strong democratic leader because he had reconciled his masculine and feminine sides.

Conclusion

In a broad sense, one can surmise that it was the positive impact women had on Lincoln that helped form him. Through those relationships involving hardship, loss, rejection, and compromise, the women in Lincoln's life provided a necessary balance. We do better not to revere him but to understand him and consider his relevance as an image and as a model. Perhaps because of his ability to recognize and utilize both masculine and feminine qualities in his character and conduct, Lincoln became and remains the role model for democratic leadership.

The full extent of the complicated relationships that Lincoln experienced with the women in his life can never be fully understood. Too little documentary evidence survives, and Lincoln, a notoriously "shut-mouthed" man about all personal matters, seldom confided his feelings to even his closest friends.

But something in his character and his relationships molded Lincoln into a human being little like his contemporary males. His sensitivity set him apart as distinctly as his eloquence and intellect.

Surely the women in his life helped create that personality. The answer can never be definitely supplied, but the question remains worth asking.

Notes

1. Speed, 19.
2. *Collected Works of Abraham Lincoln,* 1:305.
3. Ibid., 6:16–17.
4. Ibid., 8:116–17. It takes nothing away from Mrs. Bixby's loss that only two of her sons were killed in battle. One other was honorably discharged, one deserted, and one may have deserted or died in a Confederate prison camp.

5. William Herndon's description of Lincoln's ambition; Current, 188.

6. See Ostendorf and Olesky.

7. Angle, 374.

8. Sedgwick, 310–11.

9. Rice, 314.

10. Angle, 374.

11. Rice, 365.

12. *Collected Works,* 5:429.

13. Ibid., 5:346.

14. Ibid., 4:341.

15. Gilligan, 164, 21–22, 30, 16.

16. Angle, 374.

17. Oates, 266.

18. Current, 175.

19. *Collected Works,* 5:346.

20. Ibid., 8:333.

21. Ibid., 2:87–88.

22. Ibid., 6:76.

23. Ibid., 6:559.

24. Ibid., 6:410.

3

Abraham Lincoln: Commander in Chief or "Attorney in Chief"?

BECAUSE more is now known about Abraham Lincoln's legal practice than ever before, historians risk the temptation to focus too much on his legal career and not enough on the fact that, for Lincoln, the law was in many respects a means to politics, his first love. It is necessary to remember that the sixteenth president is unique among the forty-three men who have served in the Oval Office: He ran for political office at a younger age than any other lawyer who became president, and he was one of the few who ran for office *before* he became a lawyer. Although he was defeated in his first effort to become a state legislator, the effort signaled that Lincoln's greatest satisfaction in life ultimately would come from working on political problems facing his community. It is ironic that the youthful Lincoln initially attempted to emulate George Washington, his first political hero, by running for office during military service. In the end, he spent too little time on his first campaign because, like Washington, he was attempting to gain military experience while competing for public office. He never repeated that mistake. Lincoln would take a different road to political success.

According to Thomas A. Bailey's study of presidential greatness, "The American people admire a chieftain who can command their allegiance, inspire them to greater patriotism, and arouse them with a challenge that will appeal to their better selves."[1] All of this Lincoln did successfully, using skills he honed in the courtroom. He never wavered from his desire to exercise political leadership. He used the law as a springboard to reach his political

---

Originally published by Mercer University Press, 1999, and reprinted with permission of the publisher from *Lincoln and His Contemporaries,* ed. Charles Hubbard (Macon, Ga.: Mercer University Press, 1999). © 1999 Mercer University Press. This essay was first presented at Lincoln Memorial University in April 1997 as part of the conference "Lincoln and His Contemporaries."

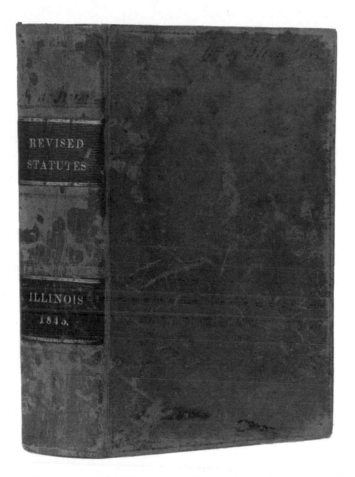

Revised Statutes of the State of Illinois, 1845. William Walters, printer, Springfield, 1845. Book, 9 × 5⅝ × 2¼ inches. This book once sat in the Lincoln and Herndon law offices in downtown Springfield. William H. Herndon, Lincoln's long-time law partner, signed the book in eight places. From The Frank and Virginia Williams Collection of Lincolniana; photograph by Virginia Williams.

goals, and this contributed to his later success as president and commander in chief.

Lincoln was able to blend the traditional differences between the law and politics into a singular democratic vision. By temperament he was not an activist like Chief Justice Roger B. Taney, who was willing to undo congressional compromises. Nor was he a lazy lawyer-president like James Buchanan. Lincoln was a full-fledged politician who was willing to find solutions to public policy issues—including the divisive issues of civil war and slavery—when Taney and others would provoke them due to their ideological extremism, narrow legal approach, and lack of political experience.

Lincoln the Warrior

Apart from showing that Lincoln did indeed adopt George Washington as a role model, Lincoln's military experience in a way encouraged him to pursue a legal career as a means to further his political ambitions. During the Black Hawk Indian War, he met his future law partner, John Todd Stuart, who later became a state legislator. Election as a captain in the state militia by his men provided Lincoln his public acceptance—a validation that he would seek continually in political life. Although the Black Hawk Indian War provided Lincoln a minimally challenging military experience, especially compared with Washington's, it linked him to a successful military campaign, even if his personal contribution to it came mostly, he admitted, in fighting mosquitoes.[2] Importantly, Lincoln's active military service encouraged him to study the law as a means to further his political ambition.

Lincoln the Lawyer

Lincoln did not practice law and then become a politician. Not only was he a politician first; he was always both a politician and a lawyer simultaneously. This differentiates him from many politicians and lawyers. There can be little question that Lincoln's long, arduous, and intensive legal career at the Bar of Illinois, along with his political career, constituted his principal schooling and prepared him for later presidential duties, including the role of commander in chief. It proved dynamic training.

His twenty-four-year legal-political career before assuming the presidency taught him six lessons. First, he developed and learned the need for unending energy—especially when considering that Lincoln expended equal, concurrent energy in politics. Second, his legal-political career demonstrated that Lincoln had the ability to juggle effectively more than one job at the same time. Third, the study of law and his work in the legislature allowed him to develop and hone his political skills. Fourth, the law allowed him to develop his ability as a public speaker and writer. Fifth, the law also gave him time to

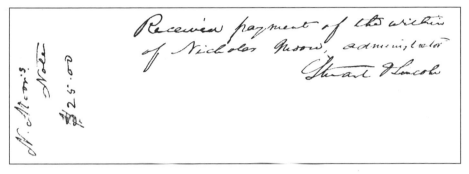

Abraham Lincoln as lawyer, autograph document signed "Stuart and Lincoln." Springfield, Illinois, 1838. This receipt for the sum of twenty-five dollars for payments of a promissory note was written by Lincoln while practicing with his first law partner, John Todd Stuart. From The Frank and Virginia Williams Collection of Lincolniana; photographs by Claire White-Peterson, Mystic Seaport Museum.

reflect on human nature and the broader purpose of democratic life. Ultimately, Lincoln's dual careers provided him the kind of broad background that assured him the potential for growth as a politician, which was always his ultimate goal. It would ensure that not only would he be a commander in chief or an attorney in chief but he would evolve as America's finest political leader. Sixth, his legal casework taught him a great sense of timing, knowing when to undertake an issue directly and when to be Machiavellian.

Lincoln's legal career demonstrated his unending energy, especially when one understands that he remained politically active. Like many successful lawyers, Lincoln boasted an abundance of physical and mental energy. He was more than an ordinary lawyer when he practiced on the Eighth Judicial

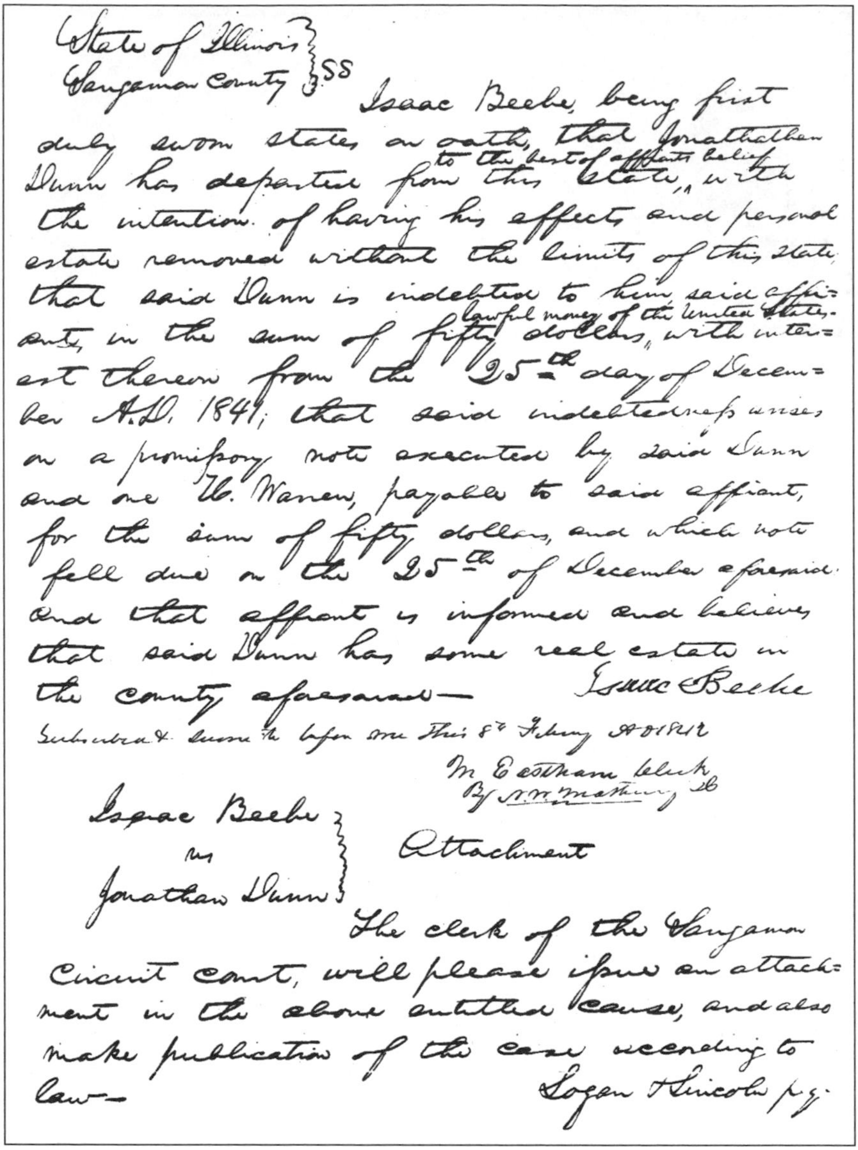

State of Illinois
Sangamon County } SS

Isaac Beebe, being first duly sworn states on oath, that Jonathathen Dunn has departed from this State, to the best of affiants belief, with the intention of having his effects and personal estate removed without the limits of this state, that said Dunn is indebted to him said affiant, in the sum of fifty dollars, lawful money of the United States, with interest thereon from the 25th day of December A.D. 1841; that said indebtedness arises on a promisory note executed by said Dunn and one W. Warren, payable to said affiant, for the sum of fifty dollars, and which note fell due on the 25th of December aforesaid. And that affiant is informed and believes that said Dunn has some real estate in the county aforesaid —

Isaac Beebe

Subscribed & sworn to before me this 8d Febuary A.D. 1842

M. Eastham Clerk
By N. M. Mathewy DC

Isaac Beebe }
vs
Jonathan Dunn }

Attachment

The clerk of the Sangamon Circuit court, will please issue an attachment in the above entitled cause, and also make publication of the case according to law —

Logan & Lincoln p.q.

Autograph pleading signed "Logan & Lincoln." Springfield, Illinois, 1838. Lincoln's second law partner was Stephen T. Logan, one of the most distinguished attorneys of the Illinois bar. He taught Lincoln the technicalities of the law, including the preparation of legal pleadings. In this affidavit, a client of the firm asserts that the defendant has left Illinois in an effort to avoid satisfaction of a debt. Lincoln asks the clerk of Sangamon Circuit Court to file an attachment on the goods of the defendant. From The Frank and Virginia Williams Collection of Lincolniana; photograph by Claire White-Peterson, Mystic Seaport Museum.

Circuit. After all, how many attorneys, either in Lincoln's day or today, can claim a career spanning twenty-four years, handling more than five thousand cases, and appearing in over 333 cases before the Illinois Supreme Court?[3] All this and politics, too.

His legal-political career demonstrated that Lincoln had the ability to juggle more than one job at the same time. Practicing attorneys must be able to handle more than one case at a time. They must deal with different cases, strategies, and ideas. Lincoln proved himself to be a masterful juggler, handling a heavy legal practice and a demanding schedule as a working legislator and emerging leader of his party. Performing multiple tasks at the same time later would prove essential in the presidency, which requires an individual to manage multiple roles: commander in chief, chief executive, chief diplomat, party leader, legislative leader, and leader of the American people.

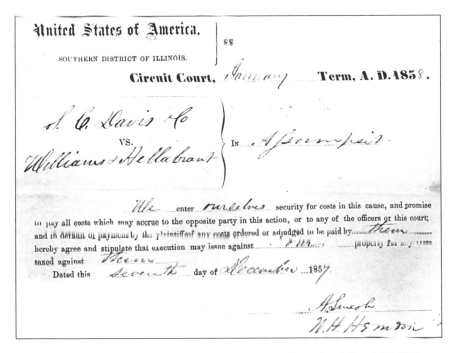

Abraham Lincoln as lawyer, partly printed document signed "A. Lincoln" and "W. H. Herndon." Springfield, Illinois, 1857. Lincoln's last law partner was William H. Herndon. In this document Lincoln and Herndon both promise to act as "security" in the costs incurred for a litigation. From The Frank and Virginia Williams Collection of Lincolniana; photograph by Claire White-Peterson, Mystic Seaport Museum.

The study of law and his work in the legislature allowed Lincoln to polish his political skills. The study of law demands skill in separating principles from facts. Lincoln did not get lost among the trees. His years of legal practice taught him to beware of stumps and to search for underlying principles. Indeed, he came to appreciate the fact that the law, politics, and life have deeper meanings. Lincoln was a complex spirit.

The law allowed Lincoln to hone his oral and writing skills. Lincoln's dual legal and political careers provided him with a unique opportunity to improve his inclination to search for the best way to communicate meaning. He never ceased working to improve his writing, including his ability to construct verse. As a result of his fascination with words, he developed a poetic understanding of the law, politics, and life. He had a philosophical disposition.

Lifelong Learner: An Autodidact

The law also taught him about human nature and the broader purpose of democratic life. Lincoln was not a specialist (few existed in his day), but he was a well-rounded lawyer with a comprehensive practice. He argued cases as varied as the validity of a slave as consideration for a promissory note, enforcement of gambling debts, seduction, guardianship, foreclosure of mortgages and mechanics liens, divorce, specific performance, county seat wars, ejectment, wills, personal injuries, libel and slander, injunction, replevin, patents, taxation, insurance, partition, statute of frauds, eminent domain, trusts and trustees, constitutional law, real estate, and procedure at law and equity. At times, he even served as a circuit judge.[4]

The lessons that Lincoln learned from his dual political-legal career can be illustrated through several episodes. His prior training and background assured that Lincoln would take a broad view of most issues and try to flesh out the facts in his effort to achieve his ultimate political goal.

Sense of Timing

As a lawyer and judge, Lincoln developed a judicious, sometimes even Machiavellian, sense of timing. He learned that some legal matters are best left alone. In a sense he probably would have been a judicial restraintist if he had served full-time on the bench.

As a lawyer who fully understood the political context in which the law operates, Lincoln learned when to lead and when to let public opinion ripen. He was the master Machiavellian in the best sense of that term, understanding that leaders operate within a small window of opportunity. He knew when to seize the initiative and when to let matters develop. Inexperienced lawyers and those without political experience fail to appreciate this crucial dimension of successful leadership.

Lincoln's dual career would ultimately provide him with the broad kind of background that would assure him the potential to grow as a politician. It would ensure that he would not only be a commander in chief or an attorney in chief; he would grow into America's finest political leader.

The Issue of Slavery: A Constitutional or a Moral Question

Lincoln's experience taught him that there were multiple levels of meaning and that a literal approach would diminish the broader political meaning of a document. For example, in an 1857 speech criticizing the *Dred Scott* case, in which Chief Justice Roger B. Taney wrote the majority opinion indicating the black man had no rights that white people were bound to respect, Lincoln fully admitted the economic, constitutional, and biblical dimensions of the slave question, and yet summed up the situation with a broader moral:

> In those days, by common consent, the spread of the black man's bondage to new countries was prohibited; but now, Congress decides that it *will* not continue the prohibition, and the Supreme Court decides that it *would not* if it would. In those days, our Declaration of Independence was held sacred by all, and thought to include all; but now, to aid in making the bondage of the negro universal and eternal, it is assailed, and sneered at, and construed, and hawked at, and torn, till, if its framers could rise from their graves, they could not at all recognize it. All the powers of the earth seem rapidly combining against him. Mammon is after him; ambition follows, and philosophy follows, and the Theology of the day is fast joining the cry. They have him in his prison house; they have searched his person, and left no prying instrument with him. One after another they have closed the heavy iron doors upon him, and now they have him, as it were, bolted in with a lock of a hundred keys, which can never be unlocked without the concurrence of every key; the keys in the hands of a

hundred different men, and they scattered to a hundred different and distant places; and they stand musing as to what invention, in all the domin-
ions of mind and matter, can be produced to make the impossibility of
his escape more complete than it is.[5]

And then came his answer to all the defenders of slavery:

> The ant who has toiled and dragged a crumb to his nest, will furiously
> defend the fruit of his labor, against whatever robber assails him. So plain,
> that the most dumb and stupid slave that ever toiled for a master, does
> constantly *know* that he is wronged. So plain that no one, high or low, ever
> does mistake it, except in a plainly *selfish* way; for although, volume upon
> volume is written to prove slavery a very good thing, we never hear of the
> man who wishes to take the good of it, *by being a slave himself.*[6]

Lincoln could reason to broader principles rather than limit himself to
previous precedents. His political values always allowed him to consider
another interpretation. His legal experience reinforced that ability.

The Appointment of Hooker: Balancing

Lincoln's ability to weigh both sides was illustrated by the way he handled the
controversial appointment of Maj. Gen. Joseph Hooker to command the
Army of the Potomac in 1863. The previous commander, Maj. Gen.
Ambrose E. Burnside, had brought an order dismissing four officers, including Hooker, charging him with "unjust and unnecessary criticisms of the
actions of his superior officers."[7] But the order required presidential approval.
Lincoln's alternative was to accept Burnside's resignation. Having long realized that Burnside's dismissal was inevitable, Lincoln had decided in favor
of Hooker, but the selection did not come without misgivings. The day after
Hooker's appointment, Lincoln confessed to Senator Orville H. Browning
that he was not satisfied with Hooker's conduct but knew of no better
choice.[8] Lincoln's most explicit avowal of his reservations, however, came
from his own pen in this lawyerlike letter to Hooker, replete with contrasting
points of view:

Abraham Lincoln

Executive Mansion

Washington, January 26, 1863

Major General Hooker:
General.
I have placed you at the head of the Army of the Potomac. Of course I have done this upon what appear to me to be sufficient reasons. And yet I think it best for you to know that there are some things in regard to which, I am not quite satisfied with you. I believe you to be a brave and a skilful soldier, which, of course, I like. I also believe you do not mix politics with your profession, in which you are right. You have confidence in yourself, which is a valuable, if not an indispensable quality. You are ambitious, which, within reasonable bounds, does good rather than harm. But I think that during Gen. Burnside's command of the Army, you have taken counsel of your ambition, and thwarted him as much as you could, in which you did a great wrong to the country, and to a most meritorious and honorable brother officer. I have heard, in such a way as to believe it, of your recently saying that both the Army and the Government needed a Dictator. Of course it was not *for* this, but in spite of it, that I have given you the command. Only those generals who gain successes, can set up dictators. What I now ask of you is military success, and I will risk the dictatorship. The government will support you to the utmost of its ability, which is neither more nor less than it has done and will do for all commanders. I much fear that the spirit which you have aided to infuse into the Army, of criticising their Commander, and withholding confidence from him, will now turn upon you. I shall assist you as far as I can, to put it down. Neither you, nor Napoleon, if he were alive again, could get any good out of an army, while such a spirit prevails in it.
And now, beware of rashness. Beware of rashness, but with energy, and sleepless vigilance, go forward, and give us victories.
Yours very truly
A. Lincoln[9]

One cannot help but notice how Lincoln gave all the positive reasons for the appointment, followed by his concerns, and concluded with both support and admonition. Lincoln's political-legal experience had taught him to take reasonable risks and to deal best with what he had at the moment. This letter to Hooker also demonstrates excellent personnel management skills that are indispensable to leadership. The subsequent disastrous battle of Chancellorsville notwithstanding, the letter had the desired result. "That is just such a letter as a father might write to his son. It is a beautiful letter," said Hooker to a friend when he received Lincoln's letter. "After I have got to Richmond, I shall give that letter to you to have published."[10] To that end he went to work energetically, reorganizing the Army of the Potomac. Depleted ranks were filled, strenuous drill was instituted, and damaged morale was restored. By April 1863, the troops were ready for the offensive. Unfortunately, Robert E. Lee was ready for Hooker at Chancellorsville.

The Case of Meade: Retaining Composure

When Gen. George Gordon Meade telegraphed the news of Lee's crossing the Potomac to Henry W. Halleck on July 14, 1863, the general in chief replied that "the escape of Lee's army without another battle has created great dissatisfaction in the mind of the President, and it will require an energetic pursuit on your part to remove the impression that it has not been sufficiently active heretofore."[11] Stung, Meade telegraphed Washington and asked to be relieved of command. In a letter intended to mollify him, President Lincoln wrote Meade on July 14:

> I have just seen your dispatch to Gen. Halleck, asking to be relieved of your command, because of a supposed censure of mine. I am very — *very* — grateful to you for the magnificent success you gave the cause of the country at Gettysburg; and I am sorry now to be the author of the slightest pain to you.[12]

Opposite. Alexander Gardner, [Abraham Lincoln]. Washington, 1861. *Carte-de-visite* photograph, 4 × 2½ inches. Lincoln's legal acumen served him well as president, especially in dealing with such sensitive matters as the appointment of Maj. Gen. Joseph Hooker as commander of the Army of the Potomac. Hooker had been disloyal to his predecessor. Lincoln wrote Hooker a letter of encouragement together with an admonition of the general's conduct. From The Frank and Virginia Williams Collection of Lincolniana; photograph by Virginia Williams.

But Lincoln could not hide his disappointment, and the tone shifted:

> Again, my dear general, I do not believe you appreciate the magnitude of
> the misfortune involved in Lee's escape. He was within your easy grasp,
> and to have closed upon him would, in connection with our other late suc-
> cesses, have ended the war. As it is, the war will be prolonged indefinitely.
> If you could not safely attack Lee last monday, how can you possibly do
> so South of the river, when you can take with you very few more than two
> thirds of the force you then had in hand? It would be unreasonable to
> expect, and I do not expect you can now effect much. Your golden oppor-
> tunity is gone, and I am distressed immeasurably because of it.[13]

Lincoln began his letter with praise before relating his criticism. In another
lawyerlike maneuver, he put the letter aside and never sent it, discerning its
probable effect on Meade and the army. One is reminded of Harry Truman,
who as commander in chief would blow off steam by writing letters he never
sent.

Appointment of Political Generals:
Alexander Schimmelfennig

In his approach to the issue of political generals, Lincoln's tack was as direct
as it might have been in an argument before the Illinois Supreme Court. The
president well understood the difference between national strategy and military strategy. National strategy shapes a nation's political goals in wartime
while military strategy uses armed forces to achieve these political goals. Most
studies of Lincoln and his generals focus on the military strategy. But it is
impossible to understand military strategy without comprehending political
war aims for which military strategy is merely the instrument. It is especially
true in the Civil War, which was preeminently a political war precipitated by
a presidential election in a highly politicized society, fought largely by volunteer soldiers who elected many of their officers and who also helped elect the
politicians who ran the war and appointed many of the commanders for
political reasons.

Many military historians have criticized the political generals, citing the
case of one appointment in particular. To satisfy a large German constituency
in the North, Lincoln appointed a number of German American generals.
Looking at a list one day in 1862, Lincoln saw the name of Alexander Schim-

melfennig. When Secretary of War Edwin Stanton protested that better candidates were available, the president insisted on Schimmelfennig. "His name," said Lincoln, "will make up for any difference there may be,"[14] and he walked away repeating the name Schimmelfennig with amusement. Schimmelfennig turned out to be a mediocre general. But those who criticize his appointment solely on military grounds miss the broader point recognized by Lincoln, the perceptive "political" lawyer. The president made the appointment for reasons of national strategy. Each political general represented an important ethnic, regional, or political constituency whose support was critical to the war effort. To mobilize German American support, Lincoln had to give them political patronage.

Emancipation as a Military Measure

Another illustration of Lincoln's concentric legal and political grasp of issues came with emancipation. The problem was prodigious. Nothing in the Constitution authorized the Congress or the president to confiscate property without compensation. When the preliminary Emancipation Proclamation was issued on September 22, 1862, declaring slaves in the states still in rebellion to be free as of January 1, the constitutional basis of the action seemed obscure. Lincoln cited two confiscation acts of Congress for justification.[15] Occupying a large part of the proclamation, they had little to do with the subject, indicating that Lincoln had not really settled in his own mind the issue of his power to act. But when the time came for the final Emancipation Proclamation on New Year's Day 1863, Lincoln had determined that his act was a war measure taken as commander in chief to weaken the enemy.

> Now, therefore, I, Abraham Lincoln, President of the United States, by virtue of the power in me vested as Commander in-Chief, of the Army and Navy of the United States in time of actual armed rebellion against authority and government of the United States, and as a fit and necessary war measure for suppressing said rebellion, do, . . . order and declare that all persons held as slaves within said designated States, and parts of States, are, and henceforward shall be free.[16]

The proclamation may have had all "the moral grandeur of a bill of lading,"[17] as one historian complained, but the basic legal argument for the validity of his action could be understood by everyone. And his sense of timing was perfect. To James Conkling, a critic, he wrote, "You dislike the emancipation proclamation; and, perhaps, would have it retracted. You say it is unconstitutional—I think differently. I think the constitution invests its commander-in-chief, with the law of war, in time of war. The most that can be said, if so much, is, that slaves are property. Is there—has there ever been—any question that by the law of war, property, both of enemies and friends, may be taken when needed? And is it not needed whenever taking it, helps us, or hurts the enemy?"[18] This exemplifies the Lincoln who consistently took the shortest distance between two legal points. The proposition as a matter of law may be argued. But it is not the law upon which this analysis focuses but rather Lincoln's political and legal approach to it. Lincoln saw the problem with the same logical directness with which he saw most problems: A commander in chief may under military necessity take property. Slaves are property. Or at least Lincoln the lawyer will treat them as such. Lin-

Henry W. Herrick, after J. W. Watts, *Reading the Emancipation Proclamation*. Published by Lucius Stebbins, Hartford, Connecticut, 1864. Lithograph, 14 × 25 inches. News of Abraham Lincoln's Emancipation Proclamation quickly reached many slave families in the Confederacy. Here, several members of one family listen as a Union soldier reads the proclamation that gave them freedom. From The Frank and Virginia Williams Collection of Lincolniana; photograph by Virginia Williams.

coln the man felt differently. Because there was a military necessity, he argued, the property could be taken by the commander in chief.

Lincoln's legal logic is also evident in his letter to Conkling: "You say you will not fight to free negroes. Some of them seem willing to fight for you; but, no matter. Fight you, then, exclusively to save the Union. Whenever you shall have conquered all resistance to the Union, if I shall urge you to continue fighting, it will be an apt time, then, for you to declare you will not fight to free negroes."[19]

Lincoln's military strategy matured and eventually encompassed both the eastern and western theaters of operation. His common sense made him a great strategist, as he was clever enough to keep troops in the west who had been raised in the west and to send other troops to the eastern theater.

Henry B. Hall, *A Council of War in '61.* Engraved by Hall and George E. Perine and published by Perine, New York, 1866. Lithograph, 15 × 18½ inches This depiction of a supposed conference at the White House with the president, members of his cabinet, and Lt. Gen. Winfield Scott and other army officers portrays *(left to right)* Lincoln, Secretary of State William H. Seward, Scott, Secretary of War Simon Cameron, Gen. George B. McClellan, Gen. Benjamin F. Butler, Gen. John E. Wool, Gen. Robert Anderson, Gen. John C. Frémont, and Gen. John A. Dix. With all their eyes on the president, the scene suggests an active and engaged commander in chief. From The Frank and Virginia Williams Collection of Lincolniana; photograph by Virginia Williams.

Just as he moved to implement military strategy, he moved to adopt an extension and logical consequence of his Emancipation Proclamation. In 1863 he announced that those slaves freed by the proclamation would "be received into the armed service of the United States to garrison forts, positions, stations, and other places."[20] In this way Lincoln planned for manpower difficulties to be significantly eased by this new source of soldiers, "the great available and as yet unavailed of, force for the restoration of the Union."[21] Lincoln realized that

> to whatever extent the negroes should cease helping the enemy, to that extent it weakened the enemy. . . . I thought that whatever negroes can be got to do as soldiers, leaves just so much less for white soldiers to do, in saving the Union. . . . But negroes, like other people, act upon motives. Why should they do any thing for us, if we will do nothing for them? If they stake their lives for us, they must be prompted by the strongest motive—even the promise of freedom. And the promise being made, must be kept.[22]

Lincoln correctly believed that the program weakened the enemy psychologically. He thought that "the bare sight of fifty thousand armed, and drilled black soldiers on the banks of the Mississippi, would end the rebellion at once."[23] He did not believe that the rebellion could survive if such a black military force could "take shape, and grow, and thrive, in the South."[24]

The Doctrine of Necessity: No Hamlet

Lincoln supported a doctrine of necessity. In his view, the civil courts were powerless to deal with individual insurrectionists. Lincoln noted, "He who dissuades one man from volunteering, or induces one soldier to desert, weakens the Union cause as much as he who kills a Union soldier in battle. Yet this dissuasion, or inducement, may be so conducted as to be no defined crime of which any civil court would take cognizance."[25] He knew that a president had to act.

In his most famous passage on the subject, he stated, as if writing a brief, "Must I shoot a simple-minded soldier boy who deserts, while I must not touch a hair of a wiley agitator who induces him to desert? This is none the less injurious when effected by getting a father, or brother, or friend into a public meeting, and there working upon his feelings, till he is persuaded to write the soldier boy, that he is fighting in a bad cause, for a wicked administration of a contemptable government, too weak to arrest and punish him if he shall desert. I think that in such a case, to silence the agitator, and save the boy, is not only constitutional, but, withal, a great mercy."[26]

Lincoln's legal arguments on the power of necessity in wartime can be found in his notes to guide Gen. Benjamin F. Butler in the occupation of Norfolk. Lincoln's legalistic view was that "[n]othing justifies the suspending of the civil by the military authority, but military necessity, and of the existence of that necessity the military commander, and not a popular vote, is to decide. And whatever is not within such necessity should be left undisturbed."[27]

Lincoln believed he had the legal power to do that, which in his judgment was necessary to achieve a purpose. On the other hand, power that was unnecessary for the task at hand he could comfortably turn down, such as execution of dissenters. Lincoln always operated within the constraints of the law, recognizing that power in a democracy always requires checks and balances. On the other hand, he refused to follow precedent and refused to retreat to his bed and pull the covers over his head in times of crisis.

Delegated Authority in Politics and Law

Lincoln's dual career in the world of politics and law taught him essential lessons in how to succeed in democratic politics. From his multiple law partners he learned to dislike inequality among professionals. He considered each of his partners to be his friend. He treated Billy Herndon the way he was not treated in his own first firm as a new lawyer. One suspects that Herndon's admiration for Lincoln grew proportionately to this treatment, even if Lincoln's one habit of reading aloud drove him to distraction, not to speak of the mutual dislike between him and Mary Lincoln. Although she accused Herndon of being unequal to Lincoln, legal revenue was divided equally between the partners.

As president, Lincoln simply applied what he had learned as a legislator and lawyer. He would willingly delegate authority both in civil and military matters if his associates demonstrated competence. His greatest success in this regard was knowing when to command and when to delegate, what to keep in his own hands and what to assign to others.

As commander in chief, Lincoln was careful to distinguish clearly between when he was giving orders and when he was making recommendations, when he expected to be obeyed and when he merely wished his views to be considered. In giving a military analysis to Gen. Don Carlos Buell, he said, "I have not offered, and do not now offer them as orders; and while I am glad to have them respectfully considered, I would blame you to follow them contrary to your own clear judgment—unless I should put them in the form of orders."[28] This is almost like an attorney cajoling, rather than a commander issuing orders.

As commander in chief, Lincoln was not perfect. The very type of suggestions made to General Buell would sometimes land him in trouble; they were not free from ambiguity. He sometimes allowed his generals too much discretion in putting plans into action, and he did nothing when some of them casually ignored his directives. Caving in to political pressures, he often meddled at the wrong time.

Yet no one could fault Lincoln's analytical thinking. On July 1, 1854, he wrote,

> If A. can prove, however conclusively, that he may, of right, enslave B.—why may not B. snatch the same argument, and prove equally, that he may enslave A?—You say A. is white, and B. is black. It is *color,* then; the lighter, having the right to enslave the darker? Take care. By this rule, you are to be slave to the first man you meet, with a fairer skin than your own. You do not mean *color* exactly?—You mean the whites are *intellectually* the superiors of the blacks, and, therefore have the right to enslave them? Take care again. By this rule, you are to be slave to the first man you meet, with an intellect superior to your own.[29]

Compare this with his letter to Buell on January 13, 1862, written while Gen. George B. McClellan was ill:

> I state my general idea of this war to be that we have the *greater* numbers, and the enemy has the *greater* facility of concentrating forces upon points of collision; that we must fail, unless we can find some way of making *our* advantage an over-match for *his;* and that this can only be done by menacing him with superior forces at *different* points, at the *same* time; so that we can safely attack, one, or both, if he makes no change; and if he *weakens* one to *strengthen* the other, forbear to attack the strengthened one, but seize, and hold the weakened one, gaining so much.[30]

Abraham Lincoln, autographed telegram. Washington, September 28, 1861. The president's concern about the crisis in border state Missouri is obvious in this telegram to a friend in St. Louis. Lincoln would often telegraph officers and civilians, asking, "What news?" His ability to convey his questions succinctly was another attribute acquired from the practice of law. From The Frank and Virginia Williams Collection of Lincolniana; photograph by Claire White-Peterson, Mystic Seaport Museum.

Both letters are excellent examples of Lincoln's formal analytical way of thinking.

Finally he found Ulysses S. Grant, a general who needed neither suggestions nor orders. Grant understood that he must not infringe on the authority of the president. When one of his first meetings as commanding general produced deadlock with Secretary of War Stanton, Stanton warned that he would have to take Grant to the president. Grant agreed and acknowledged that the president outranked both of them.[51] President and general had already established the proprieties of their relationship. "All [I] had wanted," Lincoln told him at their first private interview, "and had ever wanted was someone who would take responsibility and act, and call on [me] for all the assistance needed, pledging [myself] to use all the powers of government in rendering such assistance."[32] Nonetheless, the president did not depend on a formal system of delegation to subordinates, even those whom he trusted. On the great matters of public policy, Lincoln left no doubt that he was in charge. In September 1861, John C. Frémont, commander of Union forces in the border state of Missouri, proclaimed martial law in the state and declared the slaves of all Confederate sympathizers there free. Gen. David Hunter did the same the following spring in the Department of the South—the states of South Carolina, Georgia, and Florida—where there were a few Union beachheads along the coast. Lincoln revoked both military edicts because he feared alienating the Southern Unionists he was still cultivating, especially those in the border states of Kentucky, Missouri, and Maryland. Lincoln considered these states crucial to the maintenance of the Union. He would like to have God on his side, he reportedly said, but he needed Kentucky, and Frémont's emancipation order would probably "ruin our rather fair prospect of Kentucky"[33] if he let the order stand.

By the end of the war, Grant had earned the president's great trust. But when Grant was in contact with the enemy, Lincoln reminded him "not to decide, discuss, or confer upon any political question. Such questions the president holds in his own hands; and will submit them to no military conferences or conventions."[34] What emerges from this pattern is another of Lincoln's fundamental legal principles—a dividing line between what could be delegated and what could not.

His legal theories of emancipation as a military measure, his treatment of his commanders, and the preservation and delegation of authority were direct and aimed at problem solving. While the problems were, of course, different from the problems Lincoln solved as a practicing lawyer, the incisive logic used in their solution was much the same. Similarly, Lincoln drew from the practice of law his incredible industry and his indefatigability. His qualities developed from his wide experience representing all kinds of people in all kinds of cases.

His letter to Gen. Joseph Hooker on June 5, 1863, while the Army of the Potomac was shadowing the Army of Northern Virginia heading north toward Pennsylvania is just the kind of common sense that one would expect from a good lawyer. "In one word, I would not take any risk of being entangled upon the river, like an ox jumped half over a fence, and liable to be torn by dogs, front and rear, without a fair chance to gore one way or kick the other."[35]

Fact Finding: The Legal Mind

Lincoln absorbed information by using lawyerlike interrogatories. When he sought the advice of Gen. Winfield Scott on the Fort Sumter crisis, he told the general, "You will much oblige me by giving answers, in writing, to the following interrogatories." He proceeded to ask three questions: "How long could the fort hold out without supplies or reinforcements? Could these things be supplied within that time, and what help would be needed to do this?" These followed his law office technique to the point that he customarily finished his questions, as he did here, by asking the witness to tell him whatever else he knew about the matter. He told the old general, "Please answer these, adding such statements, information, and counsel as your great skill and experience may suggest."[36]

When his plan of attack differed from that of General McClellan's, he directed him to answer a series of very direct questions: "Wherein is a victory *more certain* by your plan than mine?"[37] He underlined his key words just as he had in his legal interrogatories years before.

He used the same approach in face-to-face contacts. After the battle of Antietam, Lincoln moved discreetly to see if McClellan was involved in any scheme to replace him as president. There had been such rumors in the army because Lincoln was to issue an Emancipation Proclamation. McClellan in turn wondered about the president's support of him, as Lincoln had sent only meager congratulations after the battle. So McClellan sent Allan Pinkerton, his chief of intelligence, to the White House, thinking he could ferret information out of the president. From Pinkerton, Lincoln learned a great deal more than the intelligence chief thought he was revealing. Using cross-examination techniques which he had perfected at the bar, Lincoln quizzed Pinkerton in an unobtrusive manner until he had convinced himself that Antietam had been not a great victory but a lost opportunity.[38]

Sometimes he had to render an actual legal opinion. There is no finer example of Lincoln acting as lawyer-judge than his review of the sentences of 303 Sioux who had been condemned to be hanged for their alleged role in the Minnesota uprising. Even though the verdicts were received enthusiastically throughout Minnesota, Lincoln was determined to separate the murderers and rapists from those who had simply joined in the battles. Reviewing each case, he found much of the evidence to be insufficient. The president

narrowed the list to thirty-eight, writing each condemned Indian's name in his scrupulously careful decision.[39]

Conclusion

Commenting on the power of colonial lawyers at the time of our revolution, Edmund Burke declared: "This study [of law] renders men acute, inquisitive, dexterous, prompt in attack, ready in defense, full of resources. No other profession is more closely connected with actual life than the law. It concerns the highest of all temporal interests of man—property, reputation, the peace of all families, the arbitrations and peace of nations, liberty, life even, and the very foundations of society."[40] It is from this mold that Lincoln was formed. Burke understood the interplay of legal training and political practice. Lincoln's life perfected the mold. There is much evidence for celebrating Lincoln as a triumphant war leader. Certainly he was more effective in his last year than in his first.

If it were not so sad, it would be almost ludicrous to believe that in the midst of his problems, Lincoln pored over the pages of Henry W. Halleck's translation of Jomini while his capital slept. And what was the result? In 1864, when he appointed Grant to command the armies, he told Grant, "I neither ask nor desire to know anything of your plans. Take the responsibility and act, and call on me for assistance."[41] He had learned that no man is a born strategist.

What made Lincoln a successful commander in chief was his constitutional "bending" within the framework of his wise, honest, restrained, inspirational temperament. He avoided narrow overemphasis and understood the difference between distortion and clarification for a higher purpose—that of preserving the Union as the greatest legal entity ever devised. As chief magistrate and commander in chief, Lincoln alternately encouraged the

Opposite. Photographer unknown, Maj. Gen. George Brinton McClellan. Published by Charles D. Fredricks and Co., New York, undated. *Carte-de-visite,* 4 × 2¼ inches. McClellan was probably Lincoln's most troublesome field commander. Though talented and a superb organizer, he was reluctant to move his forces to confront the enemy, and when he did, his engagements proved largely indecisive. Lincoln learned to act as his own military strategist because of such incompetence in the field. From The Frank and Virginia Williams Collection of Lincolniana; photograph by Virginia Williams.

American people and ordered arms to fulfill the true destiny of the Union: to achieve its promise as "the last best hope of earth." This became possible because Lincoln combined his love of politics and law to become a statesman. Rather than limit himself as a commander in chief or attorney in chief, he used his background to deliver the greatest performance of his life in the courtroom of world opinion.

Kimmel and Forster, *The Last Offer of Reconciliation,—In Remembrance of Prest. A. Lincoln—"The Door Is Open to All."* Published by Henry and Wm. Vought, New York, 1865. Lithograph 24½ × 16⅞ inches. Forgiveness and restoration of the Union are the messages in this print, which presents sympathetic portraits of Gen. Robert E. Lee and Jefferson Davis that sharply contrast with the angry public mood immediately after Lincoln's assassination. From The Frank and Virginia Williams Collection of Lincolniana; photograph by Virginia Williams.

Notes

1. Bailey, 223.
2. *Collected Works,* 1:510.
3. Statistics from the Lincoln Legal Papers Project, Illinois State Historical Library, Springfield.

4. See Duff.

5. *Collected Works,* 2:404.

6. Ibid., 222.

7. Marvel, 215.

8. *Collected Works,* 6:79.

9. Ibid., 6:78–79.

10. Brooks, 57–58.

11. *The War of the Rebellion: A Compilation of the Official Records of the Union and Confederate Armies* (Washington, D.C.: Government Printing Office, 1902), series 1, vol. 27, pt. 1, 92.

12. *Collected Works,* 6:327–28.

13. Ibid.

14. T. Harry Williams, 11.

15. "An Act to make an additional Article of War," March 13, 1862 and "An Act to Suppress Insurrection, to Punish Treason and Rebellion, to seize and confiscate property of rebels, and for other purposes," July 17, 1862. *Collected Works,* 5:434–35.

16. *Collected Works,* 6:29–30.

17. Hofstadter, 169.

18. *Collected Works,* 6:408.

19. Ibid., 409.

20. Ibid., 30.

21. Ibid., 149.

22. Ibid., 409.

23. Ibid., 149–50.

24. Ibid., 158.

25. Ibid., 264.

26. Ibid., 266–67.

27. *Collected Works,* 7:47–48.

28. Ibid., 5:98.

29. Ibid., 2:222–23.

30. Ibid., 5:98.

31. See Catton, 139.

32. Fehrenbacher and Fehrenbacher, 179.

33. *Collected Works,* 4:506.

34. Ibid., 8:330–31.

35. Ibid., 6:249.

36. Ibid., 4:279.

37. Ibid., 5:118–19.

38. Horan, 130–33.

39. Donald, *Lincoln,* 394.

40. Burke, Hoffman, and Levack, 72.

41. Porter, 26

4

Abraham Lincoln and Civil Liberties: The Corning Letter

WARTIME PROCEDURES implemented by Lincoln suggest much about politics and philosophy. When the government of a democratic nation imposes harsh methods to sustain itself, there rightly will be sincere protest and criticism, and there will be slurs upon democracy itself. This criticism will endure if the nation survives. But what if it does not survive? What if it fails because of internal division, dissension, or treason? In such a case, there will be greater criticism, stressing the weakness and inadequacy alleged to be characteristic of a democratic nation in an emergency.

Lincoln faced this in a no-win position. He would be condemned regardless of his actions. If he did not uphold all the provisions of the Constitution, he would be assailed not only by those who genuinely valued civil liberty but also by his critics. Far harsher would have been his denunciation if the whole experiment of the democratic American Union failed, as seemed possible given the circumstances. If such a disaster occurred, what benefit would have been gained by adhering to a fallen Constitution? It was a classic example of the conflict: Do the ends justify the means?

Such was Lincoln's dilemma. To merely state the case in this way does not exhaust the subject, however. Suppression is a matter of degree. To use a judicious amount of it does not imply rampant brutality, severity, and despotism.

Reprinted with permission of the publisher from "Abraham Lincoln, Civil Liberties, and the New York Connection—the Corning Letter." This article originally appeared in volume 5 of the *Roger Williams University Law Review* in the spring of 2000. © 2000 *Roger Williams University Law Review*. The essay was prepared for "Above the Law? Arbitrary Arrests, Habeas Corpus, and Freedom of the Press in Lincoln's New York," in June 1999 at the "Union Preserved" symposium, Albany, N.Y. It was also published in *State of the Union: New York in the Civil War,* ed. Harold Holzer (Bronx, N.Y.: Fordham University Press, 2002).

Measures regarded as severe in Lincoln's time would have seemed soft and "decadent" to a Hitler or a Milosevich. Congress continued to sit, elections were held, the Supreme Court functioned, lower courts sat, and dissent was allowed. It becomes, therefore, a matter of importance to examine the Lincoln procedures, to perceive them for what they were, to study them against the backdrop of those threatening times, and to note the qualifications, concessions, compromises, and ameliorations that appeared in the human application of measures that appear harsh when considered in isolation.

To speak of the government as Lincoln's is partly true and partly a matter of rhetoric. Abraham Lincoln was the nation's attorney in chief as well as commander in chief. Much that happened was shaped by the force of his personality, discretion, and executive procedure. The Congress and military leaders took actions of which Lincoln disapproved.

In managing the government, Lincoln was proactive. He did not depend upon Congress; he did not take his cues from the courts. He made the presidency, to a large extent, the dominant branch, certainly to a greater degree than had been the norm. Historian Don E. Fehrenbacher concluded, "Although Lincoln, in a general sense, proved to be right, the history of the United States in the twentieth century suggests that he brushed aside too lightly the problem of the example that he might be setting for future presidents."[1]

Democratic Leader or Dictator?

"No president has carried the power of presidential edict and executive order (independently of Congress) so far as he did," writes James G. Randall. "It would not be easy to state what Lincoln conceived to be the limit of his powers."[2]

It has been noted how, in the eighty days between the April call for troops and the meeting of Congress on July 4, 1861, Lincoln performed a series of important acts by sheer assumption of presidential power. He proclaimed not "civil war," in those words, but the existence of "combinations too powerful to be suppressed by the ordinary course of judicial proceedings." He called forth the militia "to suppress said combinations," which he ordered "to disperse and retire peacefully" to their homes.[3] Congress is constitutionally empowered to declare war, but suppression of rebellion has been recognized as an executive function, for which the prerogative of setting aside civil procedures has been placed in the president's hands. In this initial phase Lincoln also proclaimed a blockade, suspended the habeas corpus rights, increased the size of the regular army, and authorized the expenditure of government money without congressional appropriation. He made far-reaching decisions and commitments while Congress was not in session, and he did so without public polls. Lincoln knew he had the support of Congress, if not of the people. He put necessity above popularity and suffered for it in the 1862 elections. The verdict of history is that Lincoln's use of power did not constitute abuse. Every survey of historians ranks Lincoln first among the great presidents, though he would not have fared as well had the war been lost.[4]

By the time of his inauguration on March 4, 1861, seven Southern states had already seceded from the Union. But Lincoln played a waiting game and made no preparation for the use of force until he sent provisions to Fort Sumter in Charleston Harbor a month later, precipitating its bombardment by the rebels. The situation was unstable.

Now began Lincoln's period of executive action. Congress was not in session at the time (nor would it meet until the special session of July 4), and it was basic to the Whig-Republican theory of government that Congress was vested with the ultimate power—a theory with which Lincoln, as both Whig and Republican, had long agreed. As a former lawyer, congressman, and state legislator, Lincoln respected traditional separation of powers. But now, he wrote, "events have controlled me."[5]

Suspension of the Privilege of the Writ of Habeas Corpus

The state of Maryland was seething with secessionist tendencies almost more violent at times than some states that did secede. Events in Maryland ultimately provoked Lincoln's suspension of the writ of habeas corpus, a procedural method by which one who is imprisoned can have his imprisonment reviewed by a court. If the imprisonment is found not to conform to law, the individual is entitled to immediate release. With suspension of the writ, however, this immediate judicial review of the imprisonment is unavailable. This suspension triggered the most heated and serious constitutional disputes during the Lincoln administration.

On April 19, the 6th Massachusetts Regiment arrived in Washington after fighting its way through Baltimore. On April 20, railroad communications with the North were severed by Marylanders, almost isolating Washington from the rest of the Union. Lincoln was apoplectic. He had no information about the whereabouts of the other troops promised him by Northern governors, and he told volunteers on April 24, "I don't believe there is any North. The Seventh Regiment is a myth. Rhode Island is not known in our geography any longer. *You* are the only Northern realities."[6] On April 25, the Seventh New York Militia finally reached Washington after struggling through Maryland. The right of habeas corpus was so important that the president considered the bombardment of Maryland cities as preferable to the suspension of the writ, having authorized General in Chief Winfield Scott to bombard the cities, but only "in the extremest necessity"[7] was Scott to suspend the writ of habeas corpus.

The Case of John Merryman

In Maryland, there was at this time a dissatisfied resident named John Merryman. He spoke out vigorously against the Union and in favor of the South, and he recruited a company of soldiers for the Confederate army and became their lieutenant drillmaster. Thus he not only exercised his constitutional right to disagree with what the government was doing but engaged in raising an armed group to attack and destroy the government. This young man's actions precipitated legal conflict between the president and the chief justice of the United States, Roger B. Taney. On May 25, 1861, Merryman was arrested by the military and lodged in Fort McHenry, Baltimore, for various alleged acts of treason. Shortly after his arrest, his counsel sought a writ of habeas corpus from Taney, alleging that Merryman was being illegally held at Fort McHenry. Taney, already infamous for *Dred Scott*,[8] took jurisdiction as a circuit judge. On Sunday, May 26, 1861, Taney issued a writ to Fort Commander George Cadwalader, directing him to produce Merryman before the Supreme Court the next day at 11:00 A.M. Cadwalader respectfully refused on the ground that President Lincoln had authorized the suspension of the writ of habeas corpus. To Taney, this was blasphemy. He immediately issued an attachment for Cadwalader for contempt. The marshal could not enter the fort to serve the attachment, so the old justice, recognizing the impossibility of enforcing his order, settled back and produced the now-famous opinion *Ex Parte Merryman*.[9]

Notwithstanding the fact that he was in his eighty-fifth year, the chief justice vigorously defended the power of Congress alone to suspend the right to the writ of habeas corpus. He took this position in part because permissible suspension was in article 1, section 9 of the Constitution, the section describing congressional powers. He ignored the fact that it was placed there by the Committee on Drafting at the Constitutional Convention in 1787 as a matter of form, not substance. Nowhere did he acknowledge that a rebellion was in progress and that the fate of the nation was at stake. Taney missed the crucial point made in the draft of Lincoln's report to Congress on July 4:

> The whole of the laws which were required to be faithfully executed, were being resisted . . . in nearly one-third of the States. Must they be allowed to finally fail of execution, . . . are all the laws *but one,* to go unexecuted, and the government itself go to pieces, lest that one be violated?[10]

This was Lincoln at his lawyer and politician best.

By addressing Congress, Lincoln ignored Taney. Nothing more was done about Merryman at the time. Released from custody, he disappeared. On March 3, 1861, Congress resolved the ambiguity in the Constitution and permitted the president the right to suspend the writ while the rebellion continued.

Not least is the sense that we get, in a case like *Merryman,* of what a clash between the executive and the judiciary is actually like. This provides a healthy reminder of how much we usually rely, in the last resort, on executive submission in upholding the rule of law, as it is the executive branch which, under the Constitution, is responsible for enforcing the laws.

Nevertheless, five years later (after the Union victory and with a Lincoln appointee—Salmon P. Chase—as chief justice), the Supreme Court reached essentially the same conclusion as Taney in a case called *Ex Parte Milligan*. "The Constitution of the United States is a law for rulers and people, equally in war and in peace. . . . The Government, within the Constitution, has all the powers granted to it, which are necessary to preserve its existence."[11] Habeas corpus could be suspended, but only by Congress; and even then, the majority said, civilians could not be held by the army for trial before a military tribunal, where civil courts were functioning, not even if the charge was fomenting an armed uprising in a time of civil war.

Lincoln never denied that he had stretched his presidential power. "These measures," he declared, "whether strictly legal or not, were ventured upon, under what appeared to be a popular demand, and a public necessity; trusting, then as now, that Congress would readily ratify them."[12] Lincoln thus confronted Congress with a *fait accompli*. It was a case of a president deliberately exercising legislative power and then seeking congressional ratification after the event. Some, especially Democrats, adamantly believed that in doing so he had exceeded his authority.

The Supreme Court Sustains the President in the *Prize Cases*

The judiciary was allowed to speak to the constitutional issues. These constitutional questions—the validity of initial war measures, the legal nature of the conflict, Lincoln's assumption of war power—came before the Supreme Court in one of the classic cases heard by that tribunal. The decision in the *Prize Cases*[13] arose in March 1863, though the specific executive acts had been performed in 1861. The particular question before the Court pertained to the seizure of vessels for violating the blockade whose legality had been challenged, since it was set up by presidential proclamation in absence of a congressional declaration of war. The issue, however, had much broader implications, since the blockade was only one of the emergency measures Lincoln took by his own authority during the "eighty days."

It was argued in the *Prize Cases* that Congress alone had power to declare war, that the president had no right to institute a blockade until after such a declaration, that war did not lawfully exist when the seizures were made, and that judgments against the ships in lower federal courts were invalid. Had the high court in 1863 decided according to such arguments, it would have been declaring invalid the basic governmental acts by which the war was waged in its early months, as well as the whole legal procedure by which the government at Washington had met the 1861 emergency. The matter went even further, and some supposed that a decision adverse to the president's excessive power would have overthrown, or cast into doubt, the legality of the whole war.

Pondering such an embarrassment to the Lincoln administration, the distinguished lawyer Richard Henry Dana Jr. wrote to Charles Francis Adams: "Contemplate, the possibility of a Supreme Court deciding that this blockade is illegal! . . . It would end the war, and how it would leave us with neutral powers, it is fearful to contemplate!"[14]

Given these circumstances, it was a great relief to Lincoln and his administration when the Court sustained the acts of the president, including the blockade. A civil war, the Court held, does not legally originate because it is declared by Congress. It simply occurs. The "party in rebellion" breaks its allegiance, "organizes armies, and commences hostilities." In such a case it is the duty of the president to resist force by force, to meet the war as he finds it "without waiting for Congress to baptize it with a name." As to the weighty question whether the struggle was an "insurrection" or a "war" in the full sense (as if between independent nations), the Court decided that it was both.[15]

Lincoln's acts were thus held valid, the blockade was upheld, and the condemnation of the ships was sustained by a narrow victory. The decision, handed down on March 10, 1863, was five to four, and Chief Justice Taney was among the dissenters. Again, Lincoln was not Don Quixote. He had stacked the Court in his favor. His appointments were decisive in their votes.[16]

Vallandigham and the Corning Letter

Clement Laird Vallandigham, the leading Copperhead[17] of the Civil War, was perhaps President Lincoln's sharpest critic. An Ohioan, this man whom Lincoln called a "wily agitator"[18] found many substantial supporters for his views. Active in politics throughout most of his life, he was elected to Congress from Ohio in 1856, 1858, and 1860. Before he was defeated for the Thirty-eighth Congress in 1862, he returned to Ohio to seek the Democratic nomination for governor. In Congress he made a bitter political speech on July 10, 1861, criticizing Lincoln's inaugural address and the president's message on the national loan bill. He charged the president with the "wicked and hazardous experiment" of calling the people to arms without counsel and authority of Congress; with violating the Constitution in declaring a blockade of Southern ports; with "contemptuously" setting at defiance the Constitution in suspending the writ of habeas corpus, and with "cooly" coming

Photographer unknown, [Clement Laird Vallandigham]. Published by Bendann, Baltimore, undated. *Carte-de-visite*, 4 × 2½ inches. Vallandigham, a Peace Democrat who was considered the foremost Copperhead, was probably Lincoln's toughest critic. A major constitutional confrontation occurred after Vallandigham was detained, tried by a military tribunal, and exiled to the Confederacy for his bitter political speeches against Lincoln and his administration. From The Frank and Virginia Williams Collection of Lincolniana; photograph by Virginia Williams.

before the Congress and pleading that he was only "preserving and protecting" the Constitution and demanding and expecting the thanks of Congress and the country for his "usurpations of power."[19]

In his last extended speech in Congress on January 14, 1863, Vallandigham reviewed his lifelong attitude on slavery and espoused the extreme Copperhead doctrine when he said:

> Neither, sir, can you abolish slavery by argument. . . . The South is resolved to maintain it at every hazard and by every sacrifice; and if this Union cannot endure "part slave and part free," then it is already and finally dissolved. . . . But I deny the doctrine. It is full of disunion and civil war. It is disunion itself. Whoever first taught it ought to be dealt with not only as hostile to the Union, but as an enemy of the human race. Sir, the fundamental idea of the Constitution is the perfect and eternal compatibility of a union of States "part slave and part free." . . . In my deliberate judgment, a confederacy made up of slave-holding and non-slave-holding States is, in the nature of things, the strongest of all popular governments.[20]

Later that year, on March 25, 1863, Gen. Ambrose E. Burnside took command of the Department of the Ohio with headquarters at Cincinnati. Burnside, who had succeeded McClellan in the command of the Army of the Potomac, had failed miserably against Robert E. Lee at Fredericksburg, and he was eager to repair his military reputation. The seat of the Copperhead movement was in this area. On March 21, the week after Vallandigham's return from Washington and four days before Burnside took command, Vallandigham made one of his typical speeches at Hamilton, Ohio. On April 13, Burnside, without consulting with his superiors, issued General Order no. 38, in which he announced that all persons found within the Union lines committing acts for the benefit of the enemies of the country would be tried as spies or traitors and, if convicted, would suffer death.[21] The order enumerated the various classes of persons falling within its scope and announced that the habit of declaring sympathy for the enemy would not be allowed in the department and that persons committing such offenses would be at once arrested with a view to being tried or banished from the Union lines.

Learning that Vallandigham was to speak at a Democratic mass meeting at Mt. Vernon, Ohio, on May 1, Burnside dispatched two captains in civilian clothes from his staff to attend. One of the captains leaned against the speaker's platform and took notes. The other stood in the audience. As a result of their reports, Vallandigham was arrested in his home at Dayton, on Burnside's orders, shortly after midnight on May 5 and escorted to the military prison, Kemper Barracks, at Cincinnati. On May 6 and 7, he was tried by a military commission convened by Burnside, found guilty of violating General Order no. 38, and sentenced to imprisonment for the duration of the war.[22]

On the first day of his imprisonment, Vallandigham smuggled out a message "To the Democracy of Ohio" in which he protested that his arrest was illegal and for no other offense than an expression of his "political opinion." He urged his fellow Democrats to "stand firm" and assured them, "As for myself, I adhere to every principle, and will make good through imprisonment and life itself, every pledge and declaration which I have ever made, uttered or maintained from the beginning."[23] Vallandigham's counsel applied to the U.S. Circuit Court, sitting at Cincinnati, for a writ of habeas corpus, which was denied. This time, unlike *Merryman*, the Court agreed with the suspension. An application was made later for a writ of certiorari to bring the proceedings of the military commission for review before the Supreme Court of the United States. This application was denied on the ground that the Supreme Court had no jurisdiction over a military tribunal.[24]

Burnside approved the finding and the sentence of the military commission and made plans to send Vallandigham to Fort Warren, Boston Harbor, for imprisonment. Before these plans could be carried out, Lincoln commuted the sentence to banishment from Union lines.[25]

Vallandigham was conducted to the Confederate lines by way of Louisville, Kentucky, and Murfreesboro, Tennessee. He reached General Bragg's headquarters on May 25. Upon reaching the Confederate outpost and before the Federal officers left him, Vallandigham stated: "I am a citizen of Ohio, and of the United States. I am here within your lines by force, and against my will. I therefore surrender myself to you as a prisoner of war."[26] Vallandigham found his way to Richmond, where he was received indifferently by the Confederate authorities, and the fiction that he was a prisoner of war was maintained. Having resolved before leaving Cincinnati to go to Canada, Vallandigham, without interference, took passage on June 17 on the blockade runner *Cornubia* of Wilmington bound for Bermuda, arriving on June 20.

After ten days in Bermuda he went by steamer to Halifax, arriving on July 5. He then found his way to Niagara Falls. He settled at Windsor, opposite Detroit, where he remained until he returned to Ohio on June 15, 1864.

The arrest, military trial, conviction, and sentence of Vallandigham aroused excitement throughout the country. Criticism of Burnside for issuing General Order no. 38 and focusing it against Vallandigham was widespread. Lincoln was also severely criticized for not countermanding the sentence instead of commuting it. The general dissatisfaction with the case was not confined to the radical Copperheads. Many conservative Democrats, loyal supporters of the government in the prosecution of the war, were disturbed. Republican newspapers joined in questioning the action. Public meetings of protest were held. One of the most dignified and impressive protest meetings was organized by the Democrats of Albany, New York, on Saturday evening, May 16, 1863, three days before Lincoln altered Burnside's sentence of imprisonment and ordered that Vallandigham be sent beyond Federal lines. Held in front of the Capitol in the park, it was presided over by the Hon. Erastus Corning, a distinguished congressman from Albany. The meeting was endorsed by Governor Horatio Seymour, who, unable to attend, sent a letter stating:

> The action of the Administration will determine in the minds of more than one half of the people of the loyal States whether this war is waged to put down rebellion at the South, or to destroy free institutions at the North. We look for its decision with the most solemn solicitude.[27]

Fiery speeches criticized Burnside for his action against Vallandigham, and pent-up feeling was expressed against the alleged arbitrary action of the administration in suppressing the liberty of speech and of the press, the right of trial by jury, the law of evidence and the right of habeas corpus, and, in general, the assertion of the supremacy of military over civil law. A series of resolutions was adopted by acclamation, and it was ordered that a copy of these resolutions be transmitted "to his Excellency the President of the United States, with the assurance of this meeting of their hearty and earnest desire to support the Government in every Constitutional and lawful measure to suppress the existing Rebellion."[28] Bearing the date of May 19, 1863, the resolutions were addressed to the president along with a brief note signed by Erastus Corning as president of the assemblage and by the vice presidents and secretaries. The resolutions were couched in dignified and respectful

Mathew B. Brady, [Erastus Corning]. New York, undated. *Carte-de-visite,* 4 × 2½ inches. Corning was a well-known congressman from Albany who, upset over the arrest of Vallandigham, served as president of a local convention of concerned citizens. He forwarded its resolutions against the administration to Lincoln, who responded in a three-thousand-word document defending the administration's positions. From The Frank and Virginia Williams Collection of Lincolniana; photograph by Virginia Williams.

language, but they made it clear that those attending the meeting regarded the arrest and imprisonment of Vallandigham as unconstitutional and deplored the abridgement of personal rights by the administration.[29]

On May 28, 1863, Lincoln acknowledged receipt of the resolutions in a note addressed to "Hon. Erastus Cornings" and promised to "give the resolutions consideration" and to try "to find time and make a respectful response."[30]

There is no record that Lincoln was consulted by General Burnside in advance of the issuance of General Order no. 38 or upon the arrest, trial, and sentence of Vallandigham. Lincoln was, of course, thoroughly familiar with Vallandigham as leader of the Copperheads and with the criticisms of Lincoln's administration. If left to Lincoln, he doubtless would have counseled that Vallandigham be allowed to talk himself to death politically.

On June 12, 1863, the president sent his studied reply to the Albany Democrats addressed to "Hon. Erastus Corning & others." In a closely reasoned document of more than three thousand words, and in lawyerlike fashion, Lincoln justified the action of the administration in the arrest, trial, imprisonment, and banishment of Vallandigham and elaborated his view that certain proceedings are constitutional "when in cases of rebellion or invasion, the public Safety requires them, which would not be constitutional when, in absence of rebellion or invasion, the public Safety does not require them." The president defended the action not on the grounds of free speech but on the effects of such speech.[31]

The political instincts of the lawyer-president emerged when Lincoln said:

In giving the resolutions that earnest consideration which you request of me, I can not overlook the fact that the meeting speak as "Democrats." Nor can I, with full respect for their known intelligence, and the fairly presumed deliberation with which they prepared their resolutions, be permitted to suppose that this occurred by accident, or in any way other than that they preferred to designate themselves "democrats" rather than "American citizens." In this time of national peril I would have preferred to meet you upon a level one step higher than any party platform.[32]

Erastus Corning referred Lincoln's response to the committee that reported the resolutions. Under date of July 3, Corning forwarded to the president the rejoinder of the committee, a document of more than three thousand words. This rejoinder dwelt at length upon "repeated and continued" invasions of constitutional liberty and private right by the administration and asked anew what the justification was "for the monstrous proceeding in the case of a citizen of Ohio." The rejoinder, drawn mainly by an ex-justice of the State Court of Appeals, John V. L. Pruyn,[33] did not maintain the even dignity of the original resolutions. It charged Lincoln with "pretensions to more than regal authority" and insisted that he had used "misty and cloudy forms of expression"[34] in setting forth his pretensions. The committee was especially insulted by Lincoln's remark that the resolutions were presented by "Democrats" instead of by "American citizens"[35] and sought to turn the tables on the president. Lincoln was too busy to engage in prolonged debated. As was his wont, he had his say in his reply in the initial resolutions. So he ignored this rebuttal.[36]

Almost simultaneously, Lincoln was engaged in a similar encounter with Democrats in Ohio. The state convention held at Columbus on June 11, 1863, while Vallandigham was still within the Confederate lines, nominated him for governor by acclamation. George E. Pugh, Vallandigham's lawyer in the habeas corpus proceedings, was nominated for lieutenant governor. The convention passed a series of resolutions condemning the arrest, trial, imprisonment, and banishment of Vallandigham and appointed a committee of nineteen members to communicate with the president and to request the return of Vallandigham to Ohio. The committee, all members of Congress, addressed its communication from Washington on June 26 to "His Excellency the President of the United States."[37] The committee called on the president at the White House and filed its protest, including the detailed resolutions adopted by the Ohio Democratic State Convention. The resolutions were similar in import to those adopted by the Albany Democrats and held that "the arrest, imprisonment, pretended trial, and actual banishment of Clement L. Vallandigham" was a "palpable" violation of the Constitution.[38] The committee went on to elaborate its view that the Constitution is not different in time of insurrection or invasion from what it is in time of peace and public security.[39]

Employing the arguments used in his letter to the Albany Democrats and not departing from the principles he expressed there, Lincoln very promptly replied to the Ohio committee. He added "a word" to his Albany response:

> You claim that men may, if they choose, embarrass those whose duty it is,
> to combat a giant rebellion, and then be dealt with in turn, only as if there

was no rebellion. The constitution itself rejects this view. The military arrests and detentions, which have been made, including those of Mr. V. which are not different in principle from the others, have been for *prevention,* and not for *punishment*—as injunctions to stay injury, as proceedings to keep the peace.[40]

In concluding his reply, Lincoln introduced a new and lawyerlike proposal. He insisted that the attitude of the committee encouraged desertion and resistance to the draft and promised to release Vallandigham if a majority of the committee would sign and return to him a duplicate of his letter committing themselves to the following propositions:

1. That there is now a rebellion in the United States, the object and tendency of which is to destroy the national Union; and that in your opinion, an army and navy are constitutional means for suppressing that rebellion.

2. That no one of you will do any thing which in his own judgment, will tend to hinder the increase, or favor the decrease, or lessen the efficiency of the army or navy, while engaged in the effort to suppress that rebellion; and,

3. That each of you will, in his sphere, do all he can to have the officers, soldiers, and seamen of the army and navy, while engaged in the effort to suppress the rebellion, paid, fed, clad, and otherwise well provided and supported.[41]

The Ohio committee was prompt in their rejoinder to Lincoln, dating their immediate response in a letter from New York City on July 1, 1863. The committee spurned Lincoln's concluding proposals and asked for the revocation of the order of banishment, not as a favor but as a right, without sacrifice of their dignity and self-respect. Lincoln did not reply to the rejoinder of the Ohio committee.

Safe in Canada, Vallandigham accepted the nomination for governor in an impassioned letter "To the Democrats of Ohio." The name of Burnside was "infamous forever in the ears of all lovers of constitutional liberty," and the president was guilty of "outrages upon liberty and the Constitution." Vallandigham's "opinions and convictions as to war" and his faith "as to final results from sound policy and wise statesmanship" were not only "unchanged but confirmed and strengthened."[42]

The Democrats of Ohio carried on a vigorous campaign. The Republicans nominated a war Democrat, John Brough, for governor. The keynote of the campaign was expressed by the Republican State Convention in the declaration and proposal that "in the present exigencies of the Republic we lay aside personal preferences and prejudices, and henceforth, till the war is ended, will draw no party line but the great line between those who sustain the government and those who rejoice in the triumph of the enemy."

The tone and temper of the Democratic campaign was illustrated in an address by George E. Pugh, the candidate for lieutenant governor, at St. Mary's, Ohio, on August 15, 1863. The *Columbus Crisis* published the address in full on September 16. Pugh's language outdid Vallandigham's:

> Beyond the limits and powers confided to him by the Constitution, he is a mere County court lawyer, and not entitled to any obedience or respect, so help me God. [Cheers and cries of "Good."] And when he attempts to compel obedience beyond the limits of the Constitution by bayonets and by swords, I say that he is a base and despotic usurper, whom it is your duty to restrict by every possible means if necessary, by force of arms. [Cheers and cries of "That's the talk."] If I must have a despot, if I must be subject to the will of any one man, for God's sake let him be a man who possesses some great civil or military virtues. Give me a man eminent in council, or eminent in the field, but for God's sake don't give me the miserable mountebank who at present exercises the office of President of the United States.[43]

This extreme language, inspired originally by Vallandigham, no doubt contributed to the outcome. The total vote in Ohio was more than 476,000. Brough won by 61,752 votes at home and by 40,000 votes in the armed forces. The Republicans won twenty-nine of the thirty-four seats in the state senate and seventy-three of the ninety-seven in the house.[44]

One more formal effort was made in the House on Vallandigham's behalf. On February 29, 1864, Ohio congressman George H. Pendleton offered the following resolution and moved the previous question for adoption:

> RESOLVED, . . . That the military arrest, without civil warrant, and trial by military commission, without jury, of Clement L. Vallandigham, a citizen of Ohio, not in the land or naval forces of the United States, or the militia in active service, by order of Major General Burnside, and

his subsequent banishment by order of the President, executed by military force, were acts of mere arbitrary power, in palpable violation of the Constitution and laws of the United States.

The resolution failed by a vote of thirty-seven to thirty-five.[45]

Conclusion

What made Lincoln a successful commander in chief was his constitutional flexibility, which allowed him to bend the Constitution within the framework of its intent without breaking it. Lincoln the lawyer-president avoided narrow overemphasis and understood the difference between distortion for personal aggrandizement and clarification for a higher purpose—that of preserving the greatest legal framework ever devised, the Constitution. Lincoln alternately preached to the American people and ordered arms to fulfill the true destiny of the Union as "the last best hope of earth." He could not have done this if he had not been first a lawyer and then a president. Rather than limit himself to the role of commander in chief or attorney in chief, he used his background to deliver the greatest performance of his life in the courtroom of world opinion. In his "Epilogue" to his *Fate of Liberty*, Mark E. Neely Jr. closes by saying,

> "If a situation were to arise again in the United States when the writ of habeas corpus were suspended, government would probably be as ill-prepared to define the legal situation as it was in 1861. The clearest lesson is that there is no clear lesson in the Civil War—no neat precedents, no ground rules, no map. War and its effect on civil liberties remain a frightening unknown."[46]

President Lincoln knew and understood this, and he acted in the best interest of preserving the Union.

Opposite. Photographer unknown, [Abraham Lincoln]. Published by Salisbury, Bro. and Co., Providence, undated. *Carte-de-visite*, 4 × 2½ inches. This is a common variant of the original portrait taken February 9, 1864, by Anthony Berger of Brady's Gallery, Washington. The mourning-style oval portrait is surrounded by patriotic motifs honoring Lincoln's leadership in preserving the Union. From The Frank and Virginia Williams Collection of Lincolniana; photograph by Virginia Williams.

Notes

1. Fehrenbacher, "The Paradoxes of Freedom," 139.

2. Randall, "The Rule of Law Under Lincoln," 123.

3. "Proclamation Calling Militia and Convening Congress," April 15, 1861, *Collected Works,* 4:332.

4. For example, see Schlesinger, "The Ultimate Approval Ratings." Lincoln did well, too, in a survey of famous people in the second millennium. He ranks thirty-second behind Gutenberg (1) and Hitler (20). Gottlieb et al., xi.

5. *Collected Works,* 4:344.

6. Dennett, 11.

7. *Collected Works,* 4:344.

8. *Dred Scott* v. *Sanford,* 19 Howard 393 (1857).

9. *Ex Parte Merryman* is reprinted in the *Official Records,* series 2, vol. 1, 578.

10. *Collected Works,* 4:430.

11. *Ex Parte Milligan,* 4 Wall. 2 (1866), 120–21.

12. *Collected Works,* 4:429.

13. *Prize Cases,* 67 U.S. 635 (1863).

14. Randall, *Constitutional Problems Under Lincoln,* 52.

15. Ibid., 71–72.

16. Justice Robert C. Grier delivered the majority opinion. Three Lincoln appointees joined him: Noah H. Swayne, Samuel F. Miller, and David Davis. Justice James M. Wayne of Georgia loyally agreed with the majority.

17. Copperhead, a reproachful epithet, was used to denote Northerners who sided with the South in the Civil War and were therefore deemed traitors, particularly those so-named Peace Democrats who assailed the Lincoln administration. It was either borrowed from the poisonous snake of the same name that lies in hiding and strikes without warning or from the copperhead penny. However, "Copperheads" regarded themselves as lovers of liberty, and some of them wore as a lapel pin the head of the Goddess of Liberty cut out of the large copper penny minted by the Federal Treasury.

18. Letter to Erastus Corning and others, *Collected Works,* 6:266.

19. *Congressional Globe,* 37 Cong., 1 sess., 23, 100, 348. See also Steven K. Rogstad's preface to Klement.

20. *Congressional Globe,* 37 Cong., 2 sess., appendix, 52–60.

21. Klement, 149.

22. Ibid., 152–68.

23. Ibid., 163–64.

24. Ibid., 171.

25. Ibid., 177–78.

26. Ibid., 181–83.

27. Ibid., 180–81.

28. The Albany Resolves are in Edward McPherson, 163.

29. Ibid., 182; *Collected Works,* 6:235.

30. Ibid., 260–72.

31. Ibid., 267.

32. Ibid.

33. John V. L. Pruyn et al., *Reply to President Lincoln's Letter of 12th June 1863: Papers from the Society for the Diffusion of Political Knowledge, No. 10.* The pamphlet is reprinted in Freidel, *Union Pamphlets of the Civil War, 1861–1865,* 760.

34. Ibid., 755.

35. Ibid., 763.

36. Klement, 183.

37. Vallandigham, 305.

38. Ibid., 304.

39. Ibid., 305–11.

40. *Collected Works,* 6:303.

41. Ibid., 305.

42. Vallandigham to Thomas Dunlap and others, July 31, 1863, published in *Mount Vernon Democratic Banner,* August 15, 1863.

43. Klement, 248.

44. Ibid., 252.

45. *Congressional Globe,* 38 Cong., 1 sess., 859 (1864).

46. Neely, *The Fate of Liberty,* 235.

5

Abraham Lincoln: The President and George Gordon Meade— An Evolving Commander in Chief

PRESIDENTS and military officers must act under changing circumstances. They do not have the luxury of hindsight. Moreover, they have the capacity to develop in their roles or to regress. If one thing is certain about Abraham Lincoln, it is that he is the prototype of the maturing political leader. This essay explores another dimension—his capacity as president to act as commander in chief in his dealings with Gen. George Gordon Meade after the Federal victory at Gettysburg. His role as commander in chief is more questionable than his political functions, since his military experience was as limited as his formal schooling.

A Military or Political Question?

Did Meade miss a golden opportunity to crush Robert E. Lee's retreating army after the battle of Gettysburg? Military leaders at the time differed in their answers, as did members of the cabinet.[1] And modern historians continue to disagree. For example, Gabor Boritt finds that the general fell short of the president's reasonable expectations that he would vigorously pursue Lee.[2] On the other hand, A. Wilson Greene believes that Meade was "prudent" and his pursuit was vigorous under the circumstances.[3] As on a number of issues, Lincoln seemingly took both sides, initially condemning and later moderating his view.

First published in *The Lincoln Forum: Abraham Lincoln, Gettysburg, and the Civil War* (Savas Publishing Company, 1999) edited by John Y. Simon, Harold Holzer, and William D. Pederson. Reprinted with permission of the publisher. © 1999 Savas Publishing Company. This essay was first delivered at the Lincoln Forum in Gettysburg, November 1995. I acknowledge the suggestions and comments of William D. Pederson and Brooks Simpson.

HARPER'S WEEKLY.

A JOURNAL OF CIVILIZATION.

VOL. VII.—No. 341.]   NEW YORK, SATURDAY, JULY 11, 1863.   [SINGLE COPIES SIX CENTS.
[$2.50 PER YEAR IN ADVANCE.

MAJOR-GENERAL GEORGE G. MEADE, THE NEW COMMANDER OF THE ARMY OF THE POTOMAC.—PHOTOGRAPHED BY BRADY.—[SEE NEXT PAGE.]

Artist unknown, *Major-General George G. Meade, The New Commander of the Army of the Potomac.* New York, July 11, 1863. Wood engraving from *Harper's Weekly.* Based on a photograph by Mathew Brady, this woodcut from the North's leading news weekly offered a profile of the "new" commander of the Army of the Potomac eight days after the Battle of Gettysburg. The results of the battle had not yet been reported. From The Frank and Virginia Williams Collection of Lincolniana; photograph by Virginia Williams.

Meade's Military Situation: To Chase or to Destroy?

Lincoln had appointed Meade commander of the Army of the Potomac only four days before the battle of Gettysburg.[4] This battle considerably diminished the army's strength and command structure. Losses totaled more than twenty-three thousand, including corps commander John F. Reynolds and several brigade commanders. Further officer losses down the chain of command numbered three hundred. Corps commanders Winfield Scott Hancock and Daniel E. Sickles were severely wounded, as was the army's chief of staff, Daniel Butterfield.[5] These losses amounted to a serious reduction in the driving power of the Army of the Potomac. While the Confederate force had suffered similarly—over twenty-eight thousand killed, wounded, or captured—it remained a fighting force.

Despite hardships and exhaustion, the Army of the Potomac retained good morale.[6] The exhaustion extended to Meade, who, on July 8, wrote his wife from his new base in Frederick, Maryland,

> From the time I took command till to-day, now over ten days, I have not changed my clothes, have not had a regular night's rest, and many nights not a wink of sleep, and for several days did not even wash my face and hands, no regular food, and all the time in a great state of mental anxiety.[7]

Lee remained in position throughout the Fourth of July to see whether Meade would counterattack. He sent all of his Confederate ambulances and wagons under Brig. Gen. John Imboden through Cashtown Pass to Williamsport, Maryland, on the Potomac River, where he hoped to recross into Virginia. Meade likewise held to his positions in the event Lee were to try another assault. At sunset, Lee sent his infantry toward the mountains with A. P. Hill in the lead followed by James Longstreet and Richard Ewell. They would take the shortest route to Williamsport by the Fairfield Road and Hagerstown, Maryland. A heavy rain added to the difficulties of withdrawal and Meade's ability to confirm it.

After receiving reports from signal officers of long Confederate columns heading westward, Meade assembled his generals for counsel. Keeping in mind his overriding instructions from General in Chief Henry W. Halleck to protect Washington and Baltimore, most advisers recommended staying at Gettysburg rather than pursuing Lee toward Williamsport.[8] Meade nonetheless adopted a plan of a cavalry pursuit. Infantry would follow east of the mountains in an effort to intercept Lee before he crossed the Potomac.[9]

On July 8, Meade concentrated his army in Middletown, and for the next four days carefully maneuvered closer to Lee's defenses. Meade reported to Halleck that the Confederates had entrenched themselves in a line from Falling Waters northeast to near Hagerstown. Halleck advised Meade to "postpone a general battle till you can concentrate all your forces and get up your reserves and reinforcements." He warned against "partial combats" and promised reinforcements.[10] All in all there were about eighty thousand men armed and equipped, compared with Lee's fifty thousand.[11]

Lee had anticipated an attack and prepared a defensive perimeter with his right on the Potomac. He took advantage of every ridge and hill. His line ran northward and curved west to the wooded banks of a creek occupied by Ewell on the left for a total of seven and a half miles. Earthworks cut across all roads in the area, and effective cover was afforded by artillery on the heights. While the Federals constructed their own works, Meade made bolder plans: "It is my intention to attack . . . to-morrow," he informed Halleck at 4:30 P.M. on July 12.[12] He added the qualifying clause, "unless something intervenes to prevent it," suggesting his insecurity or realizing how unforeseen events could change plans. Meade assembled his commanders that evening. Only two endorsed his offensive plans, arguing that they did not have enough knowledge about Lee's strength and position. Meade postponed the assault pending a reconnaissance.[13]

He has been much criticized for deferring to his generals and even abrogating his responsibility as commanding general. When Meade reported the postponement to Halleck, the general in chief advised him to use his own judgment. Moreover, he admonished him not to call councils of war, since it is "proverbial that councils of war never fight."[14] On the following day, weather hampered Meade's observation, but he announced nonetheless, "We shall have a great battle tomorrow."[15] Meade ordered four divisions to advance at 7:00 A.M., anticipating that such a large reconnaissance would lead to a general engagement.

Unknown to him, Lee had decided to retreat after making a bridge at Falling Waters and after the Potomac had dropped enough to enable Ewell to ford at Williamsport. By the morning of July 14, most of Lee's men had crossed into Virginia. As an inadequate consolation, Meade could claim some success against Lee's rear guard under the command of Gen. Henry Heth at Falling Waters, where John Buford and Judson Kilpatrick's cavalry captured more than five hundred men, two guns, two battle flags, and small arms. Confederate general Pettigrew was also mortally wounded in the Union attack.[16]

Lincoln's Military and Political Situation

Misunderstanding about Meade's willingness to follow up his victory by engaging Lee began on July 4. Meade undermined his own position in his congratulations to the Army of the Potomac for its work at Gettysburg when he said, "Our task is not yet accomplished, and the Commanding General looks to the Army for greater efforts to drive from our soil every vestige of the presence of the invader."[17] Meade would later regret his choice of words. Without knowing all the facts, Lincoln read Meade's message and with darkened face groaned, "Drive the invader from our soil? My God! Is that all?"[18] He assumed that Meade wanted "to get the enemy across the river again without a further collision."[19] Lincoln no longer trusted his generals, fearing that Gettysburg would be another Antietam—where George B. McClellan squandered three days following his victory. Nothing Meade said or did could diminish Lincoln's unfavorable opinion of him.

Notwithstanding Lincoln's usually accurate instincts, his assessment of Meade's behavior was unfair. Meade did pursue Lee for the express purpose of battling him again, for as he revealed to his wife, Margaret, he would rather fight "at once . . . in Maryland than to follow in Virginia."[20] Recent scholarship criticizes Meade for failure to lay pontoon bridges over the Potomac east of the concentration of forces at Williamsport or at Harpers Ferry to get south of Lee and outflank the Confederates south of the river. Meade, an engineer, must have been aware of this option, but he obviously preferred engagement north of the Potomac.[21] This author could find no evidence that Meade and his generals ever considered this flanking movement. There was also the question of whether Meade should divide his own force to perform this operation in the event the force around Harpers Ferry was inadequate for such a mission. After all, this was not Lee and Jackson at Chancellorsville, where there was no river to cross following a great battle.

But the president's reaction was prompted by his efforts to convince his generals that their objective should be not the possession of real estate but the destruction of Lee's army. He had forgotten all too soon that Meade's mission when appointed in June was to stop and repel Lee's invasion as well as to protect Washington and Baltimore. Halleck's letter explaining Meade's mission had accompanied the order placing Meade in command. The army was to have two goals: (1) to be "the covering army of Washington as well as the army of operation against the invading forces of the rebels" and (2) "to maneuver and fight in such manner as to cover the capital and also Baltimore, as far as circumstances will admit. Should General Lee move upon either of these places, it is expected that you will either anticipate him or arrive with him so as to give battle."[22] Halleck told him that outside of these missions, Meade was "free to act" as he saw fit. Did Meade perform his duties well? Nowhere in the order did it say he must destroy the enemy army before it returned to Virginia (especially after engaging and defeating the army). Is that mission to be inferred without specific further directive? The president believed that should the rebel army go north of the Potomac it could "never return, if well attended to."[23]

Meade's interview with Brig. Gen. Herman Haupt on July 5 further undermined his position. Haupt was not privy to Meade's plan of pursuit, but his interview convinced Haupt that Meade did not plan to attack Lee, and he reported this to Lincoln, Halleck, and Secretary of War Edwin M. Stanton the next day.[24] Ironically, Haupt's departure coincided with Meade's authorization of the army's southern march with a direct pursuit of Lee to the west by the VI Corps.[25] Imboden reached Williamsport on July 5 only to find the pontoon bridge destroyed by Federal cavalry and the river swollen by heavy rain, making the ford impassable.

Halleck's messages from Washington came fast and furious—certainly with the prodding of the president. Halleck expressed satisfaction with Meade's movements on July 5, but his mood changed rapidly, reflecting official Washington's impatience. On July 6 Halleck wrote Meade, "You have given the enemy a stunning blow at Gettysburg. Follow it up and give him another."[26]

On July 7, Halleck again urged an immediate attack after he received from Lincoln a message to pass on to Meade confirming the surrender of Vicksburg. This news was also intended to spur Meade and remind him of the ideal of capturing an enemy army as Ulysses S. Grant had done. The president had forgotten that the Vicksburg campaign lasted over nine months. "Now," the president added, "if General Meade can complete his work, so gloriously prosecuted thus far, by the literal or substantial destruction of Lee's army, the rebellion will be over."[27] Meade understood the importance in destroying the enemy army. On July 5 he had written his wife, "It was a grand battle, and is in my judgment a most decided victory, though I did not annihilate or bag the Confederate Army."[28]

By July 7 Meade was convinced that Lee was in retreat. He gave up on direct pursuit and ordered his army southward, as he had intended to do two days earlier. His cavalry had not been passive either. Brig. Gen. John Buford's cavalry had engaged Imboden's cavalry at Williamsport, and Maj. Gen. J. E. B. Stuart's cavalry turned back an assault by Judson Kilpatrick at Hagerstown. Yet despite pressure from Stuart's cavalry, Buford and Kilpatrick continued to hold their advance positions around Boonsboro until Meade could bring up the Army of the Potomac.

Using Halleck as an intermediary, Lincoln sent another message to Meade informing him that the enemy was crossing at Williamsport and that the army should move against Lee by forced marches. He emphasized that the opportunity to attack the enemy army while straddled over the Potomac should not be lost. Meade bristled and fired back a brusque reply that according to his intelligence the enemy was not crossing the river and the army was already making forced marches.[29] On July 9, Halleck backed down and told Meade not to be influenced by "any dispatch from here against your own judgment. Regard them as suggestions only. Our information here is not always correct."[30]

It is hard to imagine that this was sent with Lincoln's knowledge. Technically—if not politically and militarily—Meade could now disregard orders from Washington with impunity. And "Old Brains," as Halleck was called, actually believed, even if Lincoln did not, that "to order a general to give battle against his own wishes and judgment is to assume the responsibility of a probable defeat. If a general is unwilling to fight, he is not likely to gain a victory."[31]

But the fury continued from Washington. Lincoln was deeply distressed by what many in the capital were already calling Lee's "escape." Such a term was highly debatable, but Lincoln was sure that Meade's cautious dispatches prior to July 14 sounded too much like McClellan by pointing to his difficulties as excuses to do nothing. The president overlooked the fact that Meade had ordered an advance *before* he knew the Confederates had crossed the river.

Yet Lincoln may also have wondered whether a reconnaissance in force feasible on July 14 wouldn't have been just as feasible on the day before.

But the president may have been unfair in his analysis. Ignorant of the topography, weather conditions, and the dynamics at work, he made it sound too simple. "We had them within our grasp," he told his secretary, John Hay. "We had only to stretch forth our hands & they were ours. And nothing I could say or do could make the Army move."[32] Lincoln assumed, wrongly as it turned out, that Lee was surrounded: "Our army held the war in the hollow of their hand & they would not close it," he grieved.[33] And at a cabinet meeting on July 17, Lincoln said that "Meade had made a terrible mistake."[34] His view was reinforced by members of the cabinet. For example, Secretary of the Navy Gideon Welles complained of Meade's "want of decision and self reliance in an emergency."[35] Moreover, on July 22, 1863, Stanton wrote, "Since the world began no man ever missed so great an opportunity of serving his country as was lost by his neglecting to strike his adversary."[36]

When Meade telegraphed the news of Lee's crossing the Potomac on July 14, Halleck replied that "the escape of Lee's army without another battle has created great dissatisfaction in the mind of the President, and it will require an energetic pursuit on your part to remove the impression that it has not been sufficiently active heretofore."[37] Clearly stung, Meade promptly telegraphed Washington and asked to be relieved of command:

> Having performed my duty conscientiously and to the best of my ability, the censure of the President conveyed in your dispatch . . . is, in my judgment, so undeserved that I feel compelled most respectfully to ask to be immediately relieved from the command of this army.[38]

Halleck declined the offer, but the aftermath of the campaign would continue to haunt Meade. While he remained in command of the Army of the Potomac and received a regular commission as a major general, the perception would later deprive him of the independent command he desired. Command of the Middle Military District and the troops in the Shenandoah would go instead to Philip Sheridan.[39]

In a July 14 letter intended to mollify Meade, Lincoln wrote,

> I have just seen your dispatch to Gen. Halleck, asking to be relieved of your command, because of a supposed censure of mine. I am very—very—grateful to you for the magnificent success you gave the cause of

the country at Gettysburg; and I am sorry now to be the author of the slightest pain to you.[40]

But Lincoln could not hide his disappointment:

> Again, my dear general, I do not believe you appreciate the magnitude of the misfortune involved in Lee's escape. He was within your easy grasp, and to have closed upon him would, in connection with our other late successes, have ended the war. As it is, the war will be prolonged indefinitely. If you could not safely attack Lee last monday, how can you possibly do so South of the river, when you can take with you very few more than two thirds of the force you then had in hand? It would be unreasonable to expect, and I do not expect you can now effect much. Your golden opportunity is gone, and I am distressed immeasurably because of it.[41]

John Hay's diary entry for July 15 notes Lincoln's depression over Meade and adds that Robert Lincoln "says the Tycoon is grieved silently but deeply about the escape of Lee. [The president] said, 'If I had gone up there, I could have whipped them myself.'"[42] Although the letter was laid aside and never sent, it expresses Lincoln's inner thoughts. Did he expect too much?

Lincoln's Prudence Resumes

Despite Lincoln's criticism, Meade had reason for not pursuing Lee more aggressively. His generals were almost all against it. They had seen the results of frontal attacks on strong positions. The rebel army had taken powerful defensive positions. Lincoln was correct in seeing the strategic necessity of destroying Lee's army, but momentarily he allowed this to cloud his tactical sense. He failed to comprehend the immediate realities that his officers could see only too well. His view may have been myopic—viewing the situation from the White House and the Soldiers' Home—rather than from the field.

Lincoln and Halleck shared responsibility for the troubled relationship with Meade. Lincoln was one of the few to blame Meade instead of Halleck for Lee's escape. Welles complained of Halleck's incompetence: "I have been unable to see, hear, or obtain evidence of power, or will, or talent, or originality on the part of General Halleck. He has suggested nothing, decided nothing, done nothing but scold and smoke and scratch his elbows."[43]

The problem was that Halleck and Lincoln failed or refused to see what they wanted to ignore—the conditions in the field. Lincoln told Secretary Welles that he had not interfered in micromanaging Meade because "Halleck knows better than I what to do. It is better that I, who am not a military man, should defer to him, rather than he to me."[44] The president was being disingenuous here, as he was meddling in military tactics.

One should also note that Lincoln was a much better commander in chief in 1864 than in 1863. He was always learning the job. But he was asking too much from Meade, because Meade refused to lose the war—even if he were not the general to win it. By 1864, with Grant in command of all field forces, Lincoln grew more realistic.

All too often Halleck failed to engineer communications between Meade and the president. Lincoln did not communicate directly with Meade because of previous problems with Gen. Joseph Hooker when the president dealt directly with Hooker.[45] Now all messages went through Halleck. But Halleck fostered bad relations between the field and Washington, telling the generals in the field that Washington was too political and did not understand the problems faced in the field[46] and then telling Stanton and Lincoln that the Army of the Potomac was no good because it did not wish to fight.[47] By 1864 Lincoln had caught on and once again began talking directly to his field commander—by then Grant.

To understand Lincoln after Gettysburg requires us to know who talked to him. Such confidants put their own spin on what occurred. One of the first was Gen. Dan Sickles, who complained about Meade in an effort to save his own reputation for foolishly advancing his corps at Gettysburg and thus exposing the Federal's left flank.[48] The president also sent Vice President Hannibal Hamlin to Meade's headquarters.[49] Lincoln wanted to learn more about the situation and the reasons Lee was able to cross the river. It was a different situation from Antietam, where McClellan had refused to move after the battle when he had fresh troops available. Meade did move—but with troops who were exhausted.

We tend in hindsight to assume that Lincoln knew everything. But we must put ourselves in his place. What did he actually see, and who was talking to him? Lincoln received inaccurate reports from Halleck, Sickles, Hamlin, Haupt, and others, and these colored his initial view of Meade. Not until

Photographer unknown, [Executive Mansion]. Ca. 1860. *Carte-de-visite,* 4×2½ inches. This is a rare image of the White House as it looked around the time of the Lincoln administration. In 1863, Lincoln maintained a command center here to follow the events leading to the surrender of Vicksburg and the outcome of the fighting at Gettysburg. Influenced by political and military visitors who had their own agendas, the president was not given the full and complete story of the Gettysburg encounter. The absence of knowledge of the terrain and weather conditions may have led him to expect too much from Gen. George Meade. From The Frank and Virginia Williams Collection of Lincolniana; photograph by Virginia Williams.

he received a corps commander's letter in defense of Meade did Lincoln comprehend what had occurred. Gen. Oliver Otis Howard wrote Lincoln on July 18, 1863:

> As to not attacking the enemy prior to leaving his stronghold beyond the Antietam it is by no means certain that the repulse of Gettysburg might not have been turned upon us; at any rate the Commanding General was in favor of an immediate attack but with the evident difficulties in our way, the uncertainty of a success and the strong conviction of our best military minds against the risk, I must say, that I think the general acted wisely.

Writing to Howard a week after Lee returned to Virginia, Lincoln perhaps finally realized his hasty and unfair conclusions after the battle. As he put it: "I am now profoundly grateful for what was done, without criticism for what was not done. Gen. Meade has my confidence as a brave and skillful officer, and a true man."[50]

Lincoln grew in his role as the commander in chief. Though he often became frustrated, overall he is the epitome of the prudent leader in public office, just as George Gordon Meade's performance in July 1863 was "competent, and committed to combat."[51]

Notes

1. Brig. Gen. Henry J. Hunt, chief of union artillery, praised General Meade, in a letter to Alexander S. Webb, January 19, 1888, *Papers of the Military Historical Society of Massachusetts,* 3:239; Welles, *Diary,* 1:374–75. Meade suffered from "want of decision and self-reliance in an emergency."

2. Boritt, 80–120.

3. Greene, 163.

4. June 27, 1863, Meade, 2:3.

5. *The War of the Rebellion: A Compilation of the Official Records of the Union and Confederate Armies,* series 1, vol. 27, pt. 1, 173–87. All references are to series 1 (hereinafter *OR*).

6. Meade, 2:125.

7. Ibid., 132.

8. *OR* 27, pt. 1, 91.

9. Ibid., pt. 3, 532–33.

10. Ibid., pt. 1, 91.

11. Coddington, 569.

12. *OR* 27, pt. 1, 91.

13. Coddington, 567.

14. *OR* 27, pt. 1, 92.

15. Coffin, 303.

16. *OR* 27, pt. 1, 94.

17. Meade, 2:122–23.

18. James B. Fry in Rice, 402.

19. *Collected Works,* 6:318.

20. Meade, 2:132.

21. Letter from Dr. Charles Zimmerman to the author, November 21, 1996. See also Hearn, 227–30.

22. Meade, 2:132.

23. *Collected Works,* 6:341.

24. Haupt, 223–24, 227–28.

25. Meade, 2:130–31; *OR* 27, pt. 1, 669–70; pt. 3, 537.

26. *OR* 27, pt. 1, 82.

27. *Collected Works,* 6:319.

28. Meade, 2:125.

29. *OR* 27, pt. 1, 85; pt. 3, 605–6.

30. Ibid., pt. 1, 88.

31. Ibid., 29, pt. 2, 277.

32. Dennett, 67.

33. Ibid., 69.

34. Welles, *Diary,* 1:374.

35. Ibid., 375.

36. Thomas and Hyman, 275.

37. *OR* 27, pt. 1, 92.

38. Ibid., 93.

39. Meade, 2:244.

40. *Collected Works,* 6:327.

41. Ibid., 328.

42. Dennett, 67.

43. Welles, *Diary,* 1:373.

44. Ibid., 1:371.

45. Lincoln has been roundly criticized for not using the chain of command and communicating through Halleck rather than communicating directly with Gen. Joseph Hooker before and after the battle of Chancellorsville. With all his faults, Halleck could and did act as a shield for the president.

46. Meade, 2:138–39.

47. Ambrose, 161.

48. Coddington, 339. Lincoln visited General Sickles on July 5, 1863, at his residence in Washington where the general was recuperating from the amputation of his leg. Sickles undoubtedly repeated to the president that Meade had asked his chief of staff to draft an order for retreat from Gettysburg. Daniel Butterfield told him that Meade had directed him to draft the order. Miers, 3:195.

49. Brooks, 92.

50. *Collected Works,* 6:341.

51. Greene, 193.

6

A View from the Field: The Soldiers' Vote for Abraham Lincoln's Reelection

THE PRESIDENTIAL campaign of 1864 occurred during a particularly troubled time. In fact, no election in history ever took place at a worse time. The nation had been entangled for three years in a bitter civil war. The growing dissent against an unpopular conscription policy, combined with growing public uneasiness over broadening the goal of victory to include emancipation, triggered draft riots and desertions that suggested a crumbling of national unity. Casualty lists in 1864 far exceeded those in previous years. Many wanted peace at any price. Critics, particularly Peace Democrats, attacked President Lincoln for seeming to change the war's aim from union sovereignty to emancipation.

It was almost a miracle that the 1864 election was held at all. And crucial to its outcome would be whether the soldiers in the field would be allowed to vote and whom they would support.

This is the story of the overwhelming support given to Lincoln over his Democratic opponent, Maj. Gen. George B. McClellan, by the same soldiers who had served under McClellan in the Army of the Potomac. It would take something powerful for many of these soldiers to forego their deep loyalty

Reprinted with permission of the publisher from *A View from the Field: The Soldiers' Vote for Abraham Lincoln's Re-Election* (Redlands, Calif.: Lincoln Memorial Shrine, 2000). © 2000 Lincoln Memorial Shrine. This lecture was presented at the sixty-eighth annual Watchorn Lincoln dinner at the Lincoln Shrine on February 12, 2000, in Redlands and was published as a monograph later that year. I am especially grateful to William C. Davis for making available his original source material for his *Lincoln's Men: How President Lincoln Became Father to an Army and a Nation*. I am also grateful to Harold Holzer, William D. Pederson, and David E. Long for their close reading of the manuscript. They offered invaluable suggestions. Thanks also to John Y. Simon, Stephen B. Oates, Peter Harrington, Marilyn Hopkins, David M. Rich, and Donna Petorella, who assisted in various and essential ways. Finally, I acknowledge and thank Larry E. Burgess and Don McCue, along with their committee of the Lincoln Memorial Shrine, for the chance to present a version of this essay.

to "Little Mac." The bond between McClellan and his men has no compara-ble situation in American history. John Pershing, Douglas MacArthur, Dwight Eisenhower, George Washington—none was as widely and wildly loved by his troops as was McClellan. Something like a familial bond, leaning toward the spiritual and even the mystical, bound them to their former commander.

Why did this bond exist? Was it because McClellan drilled them and devel-oped an esprit de corps? Or were they grateful that he did not throw them into combat and risk their lives? Perhaps it was simply because he took a pro-prietary interest. "The Army of the Potomac is my army as much as any army ever belonged to the man that created it," he would later say.[1] He deliberately identified with "his" men. McClellan never forgot the hold that Gen. Win-field Scott had over his troops during the war with Mexico. To him, the morale of the soldiers and officers was directly related to the confidence they had in their commanding general. McClellan had linked morale so directly to his own popularity that this characteristic became even more important than military ability. He set out to be as familiar a figure among the men in the ranks as their company commanders. Gen. John Gibbon recalled when McClellan shook an enlisted man's hand and congratulated him on the fight his brigade had just made. In no time at all, the news of it had swept to the entire brigade.[2]

That is why McClellan was potentially the most dangerous military leader in American history. I think he is the only commander since independence who might actually have been able to mount a military takeover of the gov-ernment without having the bulk of his army turn against him—at least in late 1862. It is therefore incredible that more than 70 percent of these same soldiers would vote for his opponent in 1864. Why did they reject McClellan? Lincoln's leadership style and campaign savvy require analysis.

Lincoln's Realistic Leadership

One of Lincoln's assets was that he knew his limitations. He had a realistic view about the sweeping forces of the time, saying bluntly that he had not controlled events but that events had controlled him. He once remarked, "I need success more than I need sympathy."[3] During the Lincoln-Douglas debates, he said, "Public sentiment is everything."[4] He understood the con-cept of mission and knew how to achieve an objective. When supporters of his administration protested against a new draft in the midst of the campaign

I CERTIFY, That *George Warburton* volunteered and served *as a private* in the Company of Mounted Volunteers under my command, in the Regiment commanded by Col. SAMUEL M. THOMPSON, in the Brigade under the command of Generals S. WHITESIDE and H. ATKINSON, called into the service of the United States by the Commander-in-Chief of the Militia of the State, for the protection of the North Western Frontier against an Invasion of the British Band of Sac and other tribes of Indians,—that he was enrolled on the *21st* day of *April* 1832, and was HONORABLY DISCHARGED on the *7th* day of *June* thereafter, having served *48 days*

Given under my hand, this *11th* day of *September* 1832.

A Lincoln Capt.

Abraham Lincoln as militia captain, partly printed document signed "A Lincoln Capt.," 1832. Discharge of Pvt. George Warburton from Captain Lincoln's Company of Mounted Volunteers. Although Lincoln's service in the Black Hawk War was brief, it inculcated in him a knowledge of volunteer soldiers and the limits to which they could be pushed. This experience assisted him in understanding the volunteer soldiers of the Civil War. The troops reciprocated in kind by calling him "Father Abraham." From The Frank and Virginia Williams Collection of Lincolniana; photograph by Claire White-Peterson, Mystic Seaport Museum.

of 1864, for fear it might cost him the election, Lincoln demanded, "What is the presidency worth to me if I have no country?"[5] He knew that to save the Union he must emancipate the slaves—not just for political or moral reasons but for military objectives: to use the vast resource of free black men who could serve in the army and navy after they were liberated. Lincoln also understood the men who served in the military.

Lincoln had been elected captain of his militia company during the Black Hawk War. Reflecting on this almost thirty years later, he said that no subsequent success had given him as much satisfaction.[6] He had learned many lessons about bloodless service during that experience. His thirty days as militia captain and his reenlistment as a private for two thirty day hitches gave him insight into the life of the common soldier. Such citizen soldiers formed the backbone of America's military. Enthusiastic young volunteers could not make the transition from civilian to military life overnight, and there would never be a complete transition. He also understood that the troops' enthusiasm sometimes had little to do with patriotism and more to do with an independent streak in each of them.

As William C. Davis demonstrates in *Lincoln's Men: How President Lincoln Became Father to an Army and a Nation,* the men serving under Lincoln in the Black Hawk War bonded with him as he shared the privations of camp life and the march. Likewise, the Civil War soldiers bonded with their commander in chief, as they came to believe that he had their best interests at heart, despite appointments of inept generals. As a whole, they never blamed the president. It was the Washington establishment that was corrupt and unfeeling, causing shortages in manpower and delays in the delivery of supplies and pay. And as a result, "Old Abe," "Honest Abe," and "Uncle Abe" became known as "Father Abraham."

It is difficult to imagine this happening today. Quite apart from the various ways in which the presidency has been altered, in many cases diminished, by those who have occupied the office since 1945, television and other media have stripped the office of its mystery and distance.

Lincoln knew that it was essential for the president to be a respected leader to whom the nation could turn for inspiration. Lincoln was determined to provide this. Davis believes that Lincoln was aided by his boyhood reading of Parson Weems's *Life of Washington.* While not an outstanding biography, Weems's description of Washington, Davis suggests, inspired Lincoln to view the first president as the father of a country where "Americans felt an instinctive distrust of civil and military rulers, but the family and the father on the other hand remained unquestioned and universally acceptable figures of authority."[7] As president-elect, Lincoln made his two-week inaugural journey to the capital, and Davis tells us that Lincoln's thoughts focused very much on the legacy of Washington as war leader. Lincoln pondered whether his generation would come to the aid of its country in 1861 as those whom Weems called Washington's "children" had answered *their* father's call. "Gradually, as he got closer to Washington, D.C., a change, perhaps unwitting, came over Lincoln's remarks. More and more he sought to identify himself very personally with the cause of Union, perhaps recalling the way Weems so completely made Washington and the cause of independence synonymous."[8]

A View from the Field

Lincoln Questions a General

In July 1861, after the disastrous first battle of Bull Run, Lincoln summoned McClellan to Washington to assume command of the Army of the Potomac and to succeed the aging Winfield Scott as commander of all the Union armies. After much delay, McClellan attempted to capture Richmond, only to be repulsed by Lee at the Seven Days' battle. In 1862, McClellan blocked Lee's drive north at Antietam. Shortly after this engagement, McClellan was replaced, never again to be given a field command. If Harry Truman deserved credit for upholding civilian supremacy when he fired Gen. Douglas MacArthur, Lincoln's decision to replace McClellan in many ways set the precedent. Both former captains demonstrated their political and military acuity in the presidency. Lincoln's initial dismissal of McClellan, reappointment, and final dismissal took even more strength of character than Truman's dismissal of MacArthur. Truman studied the McClellan dismissal, borrowing books on the subject from the Library of Congress.[9] Even though the Radical Republicans in Congress were urging Lincoln to drop Little Mac, it had to have taken enormous fortitude to actually relieve him of command, given McClellan's popularity with the soldiers.

McClellan's personality, ability, strategy, and battlefield tactics all have been discussed endlessly in literature and at Civil War Round Table sessions. But what of Lincoln's feelings regarding his temperamental commander? One cannot accurately explore the views of enlisted men about Lincoln without first exploring the evolving relationship between president and general and considering how it affected the men serving under them.

In January 1862, the North was full of optimism for the Union cause. Everywhere, except in Virginia, victory seemed at hand. And everyone believed the situation there would soon change because General McClellan was building the greatest army that the world had ever seen. No one doubted that he would soon launch an overwhelming offensive, capture Richmond, and crush the Confederacy.

As the winter of 1861–62 wore on, the North—particularly Radical Republicans—became impatient and demanded action. The pressures grew on McClellan, and the cries of "On to Richmond" increased. Newspaper editorials needled him. McClellan reacted to these barbs with outrage and growing bitterness. Lincoln nevertheless had confidence in McClellan and tried without much success to explain to him that politicians were a necessary evil. McClellan, however, blamed the president for much of his troubles and often was haughty and insulting toward him.

McClellan's slights and bursts of temperament did not inspire Lincoln to respond in kind. On the contrary, he told his secretary, John Hay, who was angered by the general's insults, that it was "better at this time not to be making points of etiquette and personal dignity."[10]

The president himself finally became impatient with McClellan's lack of action, though. Lincoln favored an attack on Manassas followed by a drive south to Richmond. McClellan had proposed a plan of attack that would involve a huge amphibious operation, moving toward Richmond by a flanking attack up the peninsula formed by the Potomac and Rappahannock Rivers. Later, after the Confederates had withdrawn from their defenses at Manassas and moved south of the Rappahannock, McClellan simply altered his proposal to make his new approach up the peninsula between the James and York Rivers. The general and his president consumed additional time arguing the merits of the respective plans.

Finally, Lincoln issued his famous General War Order no. 1, commanding all land and naval forces to move on the Confederacy by February 22, 1862 — George Washington's birthday.[11] Lincoln did not expect the order to be taken seriously as a program of action. He had issued it primarily to compel McClellan and other commanders to move against the enemy.

But McClellan continued to bicker. Lincoln finally told the general that if he could answer five questions to his satisfaction, he would yield to McClellan's plan of attack.

He asked McClellan:

1st. Does not your plan involve a greatly larger expenditure of *time* and *money* than mine?

2nd. Wherein is a victory *more certain* by your plan than mine?

3rd. Wherein is a victory *more valuable* by your plan than mine?

4th. In fact, would it not be *less* valuable, in this, that it would break no great line of the enemie's communication, while mine would?

5th. In case of disaster, would not a safe retreat be more difficult by your plan than by mine?[12]

In addressing these interrogatories to McClellan, Lincoln had moved the dispute into an arena where, as a lawyer, he was much more familiar with the rules. But the general answered them thoroughly and directly. His frankness surprised and pleased Lincoln. Although the president was not yet convinced of the soundness of it, he approved McClellan's plan. The general thanked him for his confidence, but Lincoln was less confident than McClellan imagined. For the moment, the president, probably out of his deference to McClellan's supposed better judgment, kept his misgivings to himself.

Throughout February, McClellan prepared for the peninsula campaign. When Lincoln again raised objections, McClellan suggested submitting the plan to a council of officers commanding the divisions in his army. This idea appealed to Lincoln, because if the generals approved it, then perhaps it had military value that he could not appreciate. The generals voted eight to four for the McClellan plan.

Lincoln accepted the verdict and, against his better judgment, yielded to McClellan and accepted a plan for an offensive operation he considered risky. But he began to doubt McClellan's ability. Relations between the two men became strained. Lincoln issued two orders reorganizing the army without even consulting McClellan and also added conditions to McClellan's plan, specifically requiring that a sufficient force be left to protect Washington from rebel attack.[13]

And then suddenly on March 11, 1862, Lincoln relieved McClellan as general in chief, leaving him in command only of the Army of the Potomac.[14] He had excellent military reasons for stripping McClellan of supreme command. With the general personally about to lead his troops into an offensive campaign, it was obvious that he could not adequately supervise operations in other theaters. The field command of his own army would be all he could handle. Some historians have suggested that Lincoln had intended to restore McClellan to supreme command if he captured Richmond.

McClellan reacted by informing Lincoln that he was ready to serve in any capacity and would let no consideration of self interfere with his work. Lincoln was pleased with the tone of McClellan's letter, and his attitude softened.

As the Army of the Potomac was moving toward the James and York Rivers, a major ruckus developed over the adequacy of the troops McClellan left behind to protect Washington. As a result, he was accused of disloyalty and even treason. Because McClellan was a Democrat, some accused him of plotting to leave Washington defenseless so it could be captured by the Confederates. Lincoln defended his general, but he did concede that McClellan had acted unwisely.

Lincoln took it upon himself to order several thousand troops about to embark for the peninsula instead to remain to defend Washington. McClellan protested that he was facing superior numbers and needed every man he could get. Lincoln replied curtly that McClellan had over one hundred thousand troops and that he ought to break the Confederate lines at once. McClellan was enraged and claimed he was tempted to tell Lincoln to come direct the battle himself.[15]

In a penetrating application of his realism, the president told friends that on this occasion he had taken McClellan's measure. The general had talent and was superb at preparation, said Lincoln, but he lacked aggressiveness and became nervous and oppressed as the hour for action approached.

In April 1862, McClellan began advancing to Richmond. The battle of Shiloh had been fought in the west. Lincoln now waited impatiently for McClellan to launch an offensive. Finally, he sent McClellan the following communication:

> And, once more let me tell you, it is indispensable to *you* that you strike a blow. . . . I beg to assure you that I have never written you, or spoken to you, in greater kindness of feeling than now, nor with a fuller purpose to sustain you, so far as in my most anxious judgment, I consistently can. *But you must act.*[16]

Another month passed before McClellan actually came to grips with the Confederate army. As the fighting progressed, Lincoln sent notes of encouragement: "Stand well on your guard, hold all your ground, or yield only inch by inch and in good order."[17]

As it became clear that he had been outmaneuvered by his Confederate opponent, McClellan continued to beg for reinforcements. His requests became more insulting in tone. Lincoln was not offended, thinking McClellan had written them in moments of stress and had not meant all he had said. Instead of rebuking the general, he sent encouragement. Lincoln must have felt a deep sympathy for the young general so oppressed by responsibility, for he closed his letter with a characteristically humble Lincolnian sentence: "I believe I would come and see you, were it not that I fear my presence might divert you and the army from more important matters."[18]

Lincoln was bitterly disappointed at McClellan's defeat outside Richmond, and he visited the general at Harrison's Landing to see for himself the condition of the troops. It was here that McClellan handed Lincoln a long letter telling him how to run the government and advising against emancipation. Lincoln read the letter but did not answer. He had already decided to withdraw the army from the James River and turn these troops over to a new commander, John Pope.

Lincoln ordered McClellan to hasten the movement of his army to join Pope, who, in command of a new army, was advancing on Manassas. In typical fashion McClellan delayed, offering one excuse after another. In one conversation McClellan was reported to have said something about leaving "Pope to get out of his scrape."[19] Lincoln was shocked.

Pope did not get out of his "scrape." He was soundly beaten at the second battle of Bull Run. Lincoln summoned McClellan and demanded to know if he and his officers had betrayed Pope. McClellan claimed the report was false and that, regardless of what he and his officers had thought of Pope, they had always supported him. McClellan reported later that Lincoln was "deeply moved." Others, however, felt that the president's reaction was more likely suppressed anger. McClellan then sent a letter to his officers requesting their fullest cooperation with Pope.[20]

Lincoln intended to give McClellan the command of all the troops in and around Washington, but first he wanted to make certain that McClellan had not betrayed Pope. McClellan's letter to his officers satisfied Lincoln for the moment.

The president restored McClellan to command of the Army of the Potomac, even though most of the cabinet opposed the move. In response to their protests, Lincoln said he felt he had done what was in the best interest of the nation at that time. He also said that McClellan was the best person to restore the army's morale and to whip the troops into shape for the defense of Washington. But the doubts expressed by the cabinet troubled Lincoln. He insisted that all McClellan had to do was to move the troops into the Washington area fortifications and command them if the enemy attacked the city. No field command was involved, he emphasized. Because McClellan still had the confidence of the army, Lincoln intended to use McClellan's strength with the soldiers until the army could be reorganized.

Lincoln was determined that McClellan's command would be only temporary. He had decided the general was incapable of offensive warfare, which was what he ultimately wanted from the Army of the Potomac, and that McClellan and his officers had not supported Pope properly. Lincoln's anger increased when he heard more evidence of McClellan's action during Pope's engagement with Lee. The president told John Hay: "He has acted badly in this matter, but we must use what tools we have. There is no man in the Army who can man these fortifications and lick these troops of ours into shape as well as he. If he can't fight himself, he excels in making others ready to fight."[21] McClellan would have been shocked if he had known what Lincoln was saying about him. "Little Mac" assumed he was the only man who could save the country.

Lincoln's plan to use McClellan in a temporary capacity to reorganize the army and train troops for active operations under another commander depended on Confederate inactivity. But Lee abruptly upset Lincoln's plans when, in early September, he moved the Confederate army across the Potomac to invade western Maryland. Obviously, the Army of the Potomac had to respond.

Lincoln pondered who should command the army in this important campaign. He offered the command to Maj. Gen. Ambrose Burnside, who refused it. The only readily available officer with field command experience was McClellan. Despite the president's misgivings, McClellan again was given the field command.

Leading nearly ninety thousand Federals, McClellan moved to meet Lee's scattered and understrength army. As McClellan approached, Lee attempted to consolidate his forces. McClellan mistook the sight of retreating Confederates as an indication of victory, and he sent similarly misleading communications to Lincoln. "God Bless you, and all with you," a delighted president responded. "Destroy the rebel army, if possible."[22]

Following the bloody engagement at Antietam Creek near Sharpsburg, Lee withdrew his troops to Virginia. McClellan informed Lincoln that his victory was complete. The word *complete* meant to Lincoln that the Confederate army was badly smashed up and that McClellan would quickly destroy it. He announced the victory at Antietam to his cabinet. He had concluded that McClellan would follow up the reported victory by attacking on the remnants of Lee's army. That would mean an end to the war in the east.

When he learned of Lee's escape, Lincoln was disappointed. Once again he tried to persuade McClellan to invade Virginia. As he had on the peninsula, McClellan delayed and made excuses. Many of his dispatches referred to the inadequate number and poor quality of his horses. Lincoln's patience finally collapsed, and in an acid telegram he wrote: "I have just read your dispatch about sore tongued and fatiegued horses. Will you pardon me for asking what the horses of your army have done since the battle of Antietam that fatigue anything?"[23]

Hay noted that the president was becoming increasingly critical of McClellan. As the secretary reported it, Lincoln kept poking sharp sticks under McClellan's ribs. On one occasion he referred to the Army of the Potomac as "McClellan's Bodyguard." The president had passed the point where he would accept excuses.[24]

Meanwhile, McClellan moved south very slowly and centered his army around Warrenton, Virginia. On the evening of November 7, 1862, a special courier from Washington arrived in camp with an order from Lincoln relieving McClellan of his command. McClellan's military career was finished. Never again would he receive an assignment.

Lincoln explained why he removed McClellan. One word dominated everything he said about the general: *slow*. He had been too slow in getting to the field of Antietam, he had been too slow after Antietam, and he had been too slow crossing the Potomac. The exasperated president concluded that McClellan had a case of the "slows."[25] After it took McClellan several days to cross a river that Lee had crossed in one, Lincoln determined that McClellan would never catch the Confederates and would never get to Richmond.

The president relieved McClellan out of a sense of duty to the country, but he did it with reluctance and pain. In many ways he considered McClellan to be a good soldier, and he liked him personally. "He is an admirable engineer," Lincoln was reported to have said of McClellan, "but he seems to have a special talent for a stationary engine."[26]

McClellan was simply not a fighting man. In Lincoln's mind, McClellan settled for strategy, preparation, delay, and barren victories. Hard, tough fighting would win the war, not strategic planning. The army had to be led by fighting men.

Lincoln and McClellan might have appreciated Norman Dixon's observation in his classic book, *On the Psychology of Military Incompetence*, that the two prerequisites for good military commanders are purpose and wisdom. "Unfortunately," Dixon dryly concludes, "the possession of these traits might well deter a man from ever wanting to be a senior military commander."[27]

At the time he had visited the army at Harrison's Landing, Lincoln had not correctly read the mood of the soldiers. He had come away convinced that McClellan "had so skillfully handled his troops in not getting to Richmond as to retain their confidence."[28] In fact, McClellan had lost support among the common soldiers. When he was restored to command of all forces in Virginia on September 2, a soldier serving in the western theater wrote, "There is Mclellan [sic] at the Potomac with a forse [sic] sufficient if ever he will have and still nothing done."[29] Lincoln's interminable patience with the general could actually undermine the soldier's confidence in the president. Private John Boucher complained, "Old Abe has got no back bone in him I begin to believe."[30] William Dunn of the Eighty-fifth New York had served under McClellan on the Peninsula, and he feared the worse: "McClellan must get ready though the country is ruined by his slothfulness."[31] On November 5, 1862, one soldier of the 133d Pennsylvania wrote home: "Some of us do not like Gen McClelland [sic]. He is not half the man the artists represent him. . . . Many of us do not think he acted rightly in staying so long at Sharpsburg. . . . We want something done."[32] Lincoln relieved McClellan that same day.[33] McClellan left his Army of the Potomac on November 10. Many soldiers wept as he rode past. "Boys felt bad," wrote a Vermont soldier in his diary.[34] While there were cheers all along the line, some who were present felt that these were contrived by Little Mac's supporters.

There was a difference of opinion between the officers and the rank and file. The further up the chain of command one went in the Army of the Potomac, the more critical the officers were of the president. The loyalty of these officers to McClellan was understandable, as he was responsible for placing them in their commands. Charles Wainwright, an officer in the Army of the Potomac, was extremely critical. He observed the president reviewing the troops "with his long legs doubled up so that his knees almost struck his chin, and grinning out of the windows like a baboon. . . . Mr. Lincoln not only is the ugliest man I ever saw, but the most uncouth and gawky in his manners and appearance."[35] McClellan himself called Lincoln "the original gorilla."[36]

However, it was during this visit with the army that the support for Lincoln among the enlisted men soared. "Mr. Lincoln seemed to tower as a giant," wrote one Wisconsin man.[37] Another soldier remembered years later, "We marched proudly away, for we all felt proud to know that we had been permitted to see and salute him."[38] "I could easily perceive why and how he was called 'Honest Abe,' a Massachusetts sergeant recalled. "He looked care-worn and troubled, and I thought I could detect a look of pity as he scanned our line. I think his coming down, or up, to see us done us all good."[39] For the first time, in their letters and their diaries, the soldiers began to refer to Lincoln as "Father Abraham."[40] This was in stark contrast to the attitudes expressed among members of the professional officer corps.

The year of McClellan was over, and Lincoln had won the first of two great battles these two leaders would wage for the loyalty of the soldiers. The other, the 1864 presidential campaign, was already beginning to take shape in the minds of the leading political pundits of the day.

The failure of Lincoln and McClellan to understand each other was in large measure the fault of McClellan, but it was also partly due to Lincoln's inexperience in military matters. In 1864 Lincoln and Ulysses S. Grant reached a much clearer understanding because Grant knew how to keep his commander in chief informed.

The 1864 Nominations

The Republicans—or, as they were calling themselves at the time, the National Union Party—met in Baltimore in June 1864. Despite an extraordinary amount of top-level intrigue in the party to eliminate Lincoln, delegates were influenced by the strength he had at the grassroots level. They were also pleased by the widespread Federal patronage, which had expanded greatly during Lincoln's wartime administration.

These preelection months were the saddest and most difficult of Lincoln's troubled presidency. He expected that he would be attacked by the Democrats, but the leaders of his own party and the party newspapers continued to hint that there might be a better candidate. After the convention adjourned, some leading Republicans continued to talk about holding another convention to nominate John C. Frémont. In August, Lincoln despaired so much over the likelihood of defeat that he wrote out a statement saying that it was extremely likely that he would not be reelected and that he would then have to cooperate with the president-elect, so as to save the Union before the inauguration, as his opponent would have been elected on such terms that he could not possibly save it afterward. Then he passed the memorandum to his cabinet members, asking them to endorse it sight unseen.[41]

Currier and Ives, *Grand National Union Banner for 1864—Liberty, Union, and Victory* (detail). New York, 1864. Lithograph, 12½×8¾ inches. This campaign poster featured portraits for Republican enthusiasts of Lincoln and Andrew Johnson, running mates on the renamed "National Union" ticket. From The Frank and Virginia Williams Collection of Lincolniana; photograph by Virginia Williams.

Currier and Ives, *Grand Banner of the Radical Democracy—for 1864* (detail). New York, 1864. Lithograph, 12½×8¾ inches. This rare campaign poster featured John C. Frémont and John Cochrane, who Lincoln feared for a time would become third party candidates in the 1864 election. The candidates withdrew from the race in September. From The Frank and Virginia Williams Collection of Lincolniana; photograph by Virginia Williams.

Currier and Ives, *Grand National Democratic Banner—Peace! Union! And Victory!* (detail). New York, 1864. Lithograph, 12½×8¾ inches. Here, America's best-known, best-selling printmakers offered flattering portraits of Democratic presidential and vice presidential standard bearers George B. McClellan and George H. Pendleton. From The Frank and Virginia Williams Collection of Lincolniana; photograph by Virginia Williams.

Late in August, the Democrats met in Chicago and nominated George B. McClellan for president and George Pendleton, a Peace Democrat from Ohio, for vice president. Yet the Democrats who supported the war had to yield to the peace wing of their party in calling the war a failure and urging a cease-fire. Clement Vallandigham, the most famous Copperhead in the country, had succeeded in getting his "war-failure" resolution adopted as the second plank of the Democratic Party platform. It read:

> RESOLVED, That this convention does explicitly declare, as the sense of the American people that after four years of failure to restore the Union by the experiment of war, during which, under the pretense of a military necessity of war-power higher than the Constitution itself has been disregarded in every part, and public liberty and private right trodden down, and the material prosperity of the country essentially impaired justice, humanity, liberty and the public welfare demand that immediate efforts be made for a cessation of hostilities, with a view to an ultimate convention of the States, or other peaceable means, to the end that at the earliest practicable moment peace may be restored on the basis of the Federal Union of the States.[42]

It was the Copperheads' call for peace at any price, an armistice without conditions and a negotiated settlement, with nothing to guarantee that the Confederacy would in fact exchange reunion for peace. The McClellan men attempted to insert a substitute plank making reunion the precondition for peace talks, but this effort failed.

The peace plank was so strong that even McClellan quickly repudiated it. In contrast, the National Union Party's platform included a commitment to a constitutional amendment ending slavery in the United States and a determination to prosecute the war to total victory without compromise.

The campaign began to look like a battle between a president who was losing the war and a dismissed general who was prepared to sue for peace.

Campaigning in the Field

Both parties appealed to the soldiers' vote in their platforms. Soldier voting was an innovation in 1864.

Veterans organizations were politically active during the 1864 canvass. The McClellan Legion was formed to generate enthusiasm and counter the fear that all soldiers would vote for Lincoln. These pro-McClellan officers made it known that they did not accept Copperheads as members and that they rejected the Chicago platform. Also quick to realize the importance of capturing the soldiers' vote, the Republicans formed the Union League Club for veterans.

To gain the soldiers' support, the Unionists conducted an active campaign in the ranks. Joseph Medill sent seventy thousand copies of his pro-Lincoln, pro-Republican *Chicago Tribune* to the army. Many editors followed suit.[43] In some units, commanding officers prohibited the distribution of Democratic literature. General Ulysses S. Grant specifically addressed this concern in a letter to the secretary of war, which, while supporting the right of "Armies in the field to vote," suggested, "Beyond this nothing whatever should be allowed. No political meetings, no harangues from soldiers or citizens and no canvassing of camps or regiments for votes."[44]

Harper's Weekly, widely distributed in the camps, reported on September 10, 1864, that the Democratic Party platform adopted in Chicago would "satisfy every foreign and domestic enemy of American Union and Liberty. It declares that the Government of the United States is guilty of resisting rebellion, and that the American people can not maintain the authority of their laws."

Money was no object for the incumbent administration. Federal office-holders were subject to assessment, not only by the National Union Executive Committee and the Union Executive Congressional Committee but by state party committees as well. These committees also solicited governmental contractors and others who had benefited from government contracts for contributions. Government employees were put to work in the campaign.[45]

Attempts were made to get military leaders to declare themselves in favor of McClellan. At one time or another, most of the prominent commanders in the II, III, V, and VI Corps of the Army of the Potomac purportedly expressed support. This was due in no small measure to opposition to emancipation, a position shared with most Democrats. But allowing one's name to become linked with McClellan could damage the officer's chance for promotion. Most officers were thus quick to declare that they were *not* supporting McClellan. This probably resulted from their fear of Secretary of War Edwin M. Stanton. An indication of this was reflected in a letter from Stanton's wartime papers in which the correspondent wrote, "You will perhaps know about the political preferences of the Generals whose names I have given you and will know how to apply the remedy better than I do."[46]

Newspapers on both sides claimed that the soldiers would support their candidates. Union Party papers filled their columns with letters from soldiers to relatives and friends emphasizing the army's hatred for Democrats and Copperheads, while the Democrats published letters denouncing Lincoln. The Union Party was so effective with its propaganda that on election eve the army seemed to have been completely Lincolnized. An overwhelming majority of all Union soldiers — 78 percent, compared with 53 percent of the civilian vote — cast ballots for Lincoln. This was remarkable because some 40–45 percent had been Democrats in 1860, and McClellan had retained his popularity with the Army of the Potomac. Many veterans indicated that while they still admired McClellan, they did not like the company he kept. At least half of the former Democrats voted for Lincoln in 1864. As one of them explained: "I can not vote for one thing and fight for another."[47]

The inconsistency between McClellan's position on the war and the platform plank on which he ran proved too great for many enlisted men who otherwise might have voted against the president. "You think perhaps I am a McClellan man," an artillerist wrote home in October. "Yes, I would rather follow him than any man on earth for I know him to possess the true principle of the Soldier and the man, but I could not vote for him it is the wrong party, that comes in power with him if he is elected."[48] A colonel from New York who had been a Little Mac supporter when he had joined the Army of the Potomac left soon thereafter, downcast over the absence of any real support for McClellan among the soldiers who had once loved him.[49]

Moreover, Confederate enthusiasm at the nomination of McClellan hurt him with the soldiers of the Union army. Southern leaders and soldiers saw in McClellan perhaps their last chance for independence. "The rebs are hollowing [*sic*] for McClellan all the time," a man serving with Grant wrote in October.[50]

Both the president and Mrs. Lincoln had shown support and concern for soldiers by regularly visiting the Washington, D.C., military hospitals. Lincoln himself vigorously campaigned among the troops in the eastern armies by visiting them in the field and by greeting them in Washington. More important were his widely disseminated public statements addressed directly to soldiers. He used such occasions to emphasize the importance of the struggle, telling the 166th Ohio on the same day he wrote his blind memorandum, "It is not merely for to-day, but for all time to come that we should perpetuate for our children's children this great and free government." He told soldiers that he himself was a living witness that any man, however humble, could rise to the highest office in the land and that the soldiers were fighting for their constitutional freedoms "in order that each of you may have through this free government which we have enjoyed, an open field and a fair chance for your industry, enterprise and intelligence; that you may all have equal privileges in the race of life."[51] The popular press, especially the illustrated weeklies like *Frank Leslie's* and *Harper's*, often ran woodcuts showing Lincoln in the presence of soldiers. Framed lithographs of these woodcuts were hung in many northern homes.

This was a time when candidates did not personally campaign with the electorate. McClellan remained in virtual seclusion, handling campaign busi-

THE GUNBOAT CANDIDATE
AT THE BATTLE OF MALVERN HILL.

Currier and Ives, *The Gunboat Candidate—At the Battle of Malvern Hill.* New York, 1864. Lithograph, 10⅙ × 13¼ inches. This anti-McClellan cartoon illustrated the Republicans' charge that McClellan was a coward, based on the allegation that he remained aboard the gunboat *Galena* while the Army of the Potomac fought the battle of Malvern Hill, Virginia, in 1862. Actually, McClellan visited the *Galena* before the battle to reconnoiter a possible fallback position for his army, which he believed to be exhausted. His defeatist attitude inspired charges of physical cowardice. From The Frank and Virginia Williams Collection of Lincolniana; photograph by Claire White-Peterson, Mystic Seaport Museum.

ness through a secretary. He stood on his record and issued no position papers after writing his acceptance letter. He made only two public appearances: at a party rally in Newark in September and at a massive torchlight parade in New York shortly before Election Day. He refused repeated invitations to appear in Pennsylvania, a crucial state in the election.

The soldiers sensed a basic difference between Lincoln and McClellan. They trusted a leader who told it the way it was. By contrast, McClellan prevaricated and tried to reconcile the conflict between his own position and that of the peace platform of his own party. A Kentucky soldier expected he would vote for McClellan, but he "could make no point" against Lincoln. "I cannot assure that Lincoln has, as yet, committed any very objectionable act toward the people."[52] An Illinois soldier serving in the West believed that "the best news is the nominations of Abe Lincoln and Andy Johnson. . . . It gives unbounded satisfaction to the soldiers."[53] These were opinions that typified the attitudes of the soldiers in the ranks. The nominating convention of the National Union Party paid high tribute to the men in the ranks, whose votes would be needed. The platform cited the sacrifices of

> the soldiers and sailors of the army and navy who have periled their lives in defense of their country and in vindication of the honor of its flag; that the nation owes to them some permanent recognition of their patriotism and their valor, and ample and permanent provision for those of their survivors who have received disabling and honorable wounds in the service of the country; and that the memories of those who have fallen in its defense shall be held in grateful and everlasting remembrance.[54]

Lincoln's acceptance letter, which was widely published, offered his gratitude to the troops, "as they forever must and will be remembered by the grateful country for whose salvation they devote their lives."[55] He meant it. "I would rather be defeated with the soldier vote behind me than to be elected without it," he said to a friend.[56]

The only message sent to the soldiers in the field by the Democrats was that their efforts were for naught and that, after all of their suffering, if it won the White House, the Democratic Party would be willing to surrender and admit defeat. One private said, "A man must be judged by the company he keeps."[57] "I cannot swallow McClellan, his platform is too shallow," said a soldier serving at Petersburg, and another thought: "McClellan is fast loosing [*sic*] what friends he had in the army and I have no doubt Lincoln will have a large majority of the army vote. The Chicago platform is more than our heroes can stand."[58]

The heroes of the army voted as they did based on a number of trying experiences which soldier and commander in chief had lived through together: the Emancipation Proclamation, the dismissal of McClellan, the appointment of incompetent generals, especially in the East, the various drafts, and costly defeats like Fredericksburg.

The Military Situation Changes

The war situation in August 1864 was dismal. Gen. Jubal Early had led a small Confederate army to the outskirts of Washington in July, Gen. William T. Sherman seemed stymied outside Atlanta, Grant was blocked at Petersburg, and Ben Butler was bottled up at Bermuda Hundred. Ben Wade, a major congressional critic of Lincoln and an important member of the Committee on the Conduct of the War, came to the president and said, "You are the father of every military blunder that has been made during the war. This government is on the road to Hell, and you are not a mile from there this minute." Lincoln responded, "Yes . . . that is just about the distance from here to the Capitol!"[59]

But on August 5, Adm. David Farragut's fleet captured Mobile Bay. On September 2, a welcome telegram arrived from Sherman: "Atlanta is ours, and fairly won." With this news eventual military victory seemed certain. On September 18, Sheridan's victory at Winchester was further cause for celebration across the North. Horace Greeley, editor of the influential *New York Tribune,* now proclaimed his support of Lincoln.[60] With that declaration, other journals followed suit.

The Emancipation Card

What effect did Lincoln's Emancipation Proclamation have on the soldiers' vote? It is a difficult question even with the hindsight afforded after more than a century.

The most dangerous subject that any leader could dare tinker with was emancipation. First, in the critical border states, it affected the property of tens of thousands of the most influential men and the social and economic interests of nearly all white people. Second, by turning it into a war against slavery, the president risked losing the public consensus which had supported the government during the first year of the war. Most Democrats and some moderate Republicans would protest that emancipation was a betrayal of the president's solemn pledge that the war would be fought only for the restoration of the Union. Third, it was feared that Lincoln's Proclamation would forge a bond between the troops and McClellan because many soldiers opposed emancipation and the arming of blacks.

To calm dissenters in the North, Lincoln reiterated his often-stated wish to colonize former slaves in either Africa or Central America, thus suggesting that newly freed blacks would not pose a social threat or economic competition for working-class people in the North. The president continued his efforts, as late as his December 1862 Annual Message to Congress, to offer delay and compensation if the slave border states would emancipate.[61]

Perhaps to prevent criticism of his document on social grounds, Lincoln made the Emancipation Proclamation legalistic, with "all the moral grandeur of a bill of lading," as one historian later said.[62] The president still insisted that the war was being waged to restore the Union. Any suggestion of a moral crusade, social justice, or equal rights would have inflamed the conservative elements in the army and at home. Yet Lincoln himself had said that once he issued the Emancipation Proclamation, "the character of the war will be changed. It will be one of subjugation. . . . The South is to be destroyed and replaced by new propositions and ideas." Lincoln's policy turned the war into the very thing he had warned against: a "remorseless revolutionary struggle" that did indeed vanquish the Old South and kill plenty of rebels.[63] The new ideas and propositions Lincoln had in mind included legal rights and limited male suffrage for the former slaves.

Nevertheless, one army surgeon reported, "His Proclamation, issued last month, has caused considerable discontent among the regiments of Maryland, Virginia, Pennsylvania, New York, and the West."[64] The officers who had served under McClellan openly ridiculed the Proclamation. Some officers engaged in "headquarters bluster," saying that the army should march on Washington to insist on revoking the president's Proclamation.[65] McClellan himself had earlier warned Lincoln against such a move.

Yet many men in the ranks received the Emancipation Proclamation with greater understanding than their officers. "I am glad more than ever that I enlisted sence [*sic*] I have read the President's Proclamation because I think the fight is freedom or slavery," a private in a Massachusetts outfit wrote.[66] The Western soldier was quick to concur with the Proclamation. An Illinois soldier exclaimed one week after the announcement, "My hopes are somewhat revived since Old Abe has come out with his Proclamation. The curse of slavery has got to go by the board and no mistake. Emancipation is becoming popular through out the whole Union every body knows that slavery was the cause of this war and slavery stands in the way of putting down this rebellion and now let us put it out of the way."[67]

The fact that Lincoln kept his promise to issue the final Emancipation Proclamation on January 1, 1863, also had an impact. One Missouri soldier confessed, "I am awaiting with great anxiety to here weather Old Abe sticks up to his sept. proclamation if he shrinks back in the least from that the thing is done and my hopes are gone."[68]

By the time of the election on November 8, 1864, emancipation was less an issue with the soldiers than it was with Northern civilians. Those who had to fight were the first to recognize that with emancipation the war was going better for them than for the enemy. It did mean subjugation of the South. To them this was the strongest weapon that the Union had brought to the conflict since Fort Sumter. James Abraham wrote: "Not only do I endorse the proclamation but endorse every other proposition looking to the overthrow of this Giant and Hell born plot of traitors."[69] Many soldiers felt anger at civilian criticism of the proclamation. An Illinois private wrote, "All of that excitement at home is working on the army and even if it requires bayonets, the good of the army demands that the agitation cease."[70] This may account for the great disparity in the support for Lincoln between the Union soldiers and the civilian vote.[71]

Who Could Vote?

In September 1862, Wisconsin enacted the first absentee ballot law, which made it possible for soldiers to cast their ballots in the field. Fourteen states followed Wisconsin's precedent: California, Connecticut, Iowa, Kansas, Kentucky, Maine, Maryland, Massachusetts, Michigan, Minnesota, Missouri, New Hampshire, New York, and Pennsylvania. On the other hand, seven states did not: Delaware, Illinois, Indiana, Nevada, New Jersey, Oregon, and Rhode Island. The eleven states of the Confederacy did not participate in the election of 1864.

States with Democratic legislatures (Illinois, Indiana, and New Jersey) did not enact legislation providing for the absentee ballot, as they feared Lincoln would prevail if the soldiers voted. This may have been due to a belief that the governmental machinery would be used to coerce the soldiers to vote for the president and the National Union Party. Democrats and Union Republicans profoundly distrusted each other, since each group had very different attitudes about the meaning of the war. To enable the Hoosier soldiers to cast ballots, Indiana governor Oliver Morton suggested that all soldiers unfit for service—many of whom languished in hospitals outside of the state— be sent home for the election. President Lincoln approved the measure.

The absentee ballot legislation in the states that permitted it followed the same pattern first promulgated by Wisconsin. First, the laws permitted all qualified electors (four states permitted blacks to vote) who were in the military service of the United States or that state to vote at any of the posts, camps, or locations where regiments from that state were stationed. Second, a number of ranking officers or commissioners sent to the units by the several states would act as inspectors, and clerks were appointed. Other sections prescribed the hours voting would occur, the rights of inspectors or commissioners to challenge electors, maintenance of poll lists, and the manner by which votes would be counted and transmitted to the secretary of state, who would then forward the votes to county boards for final tally.

Some states, like Minnesota, mandated secret ballots. These were to be sealed in envelopes and forwarded to the election districts for mingling with the other votes cast in the home district. In these states, it was not possible to know how the soldiers voted.

Republicans were quick to claim that they alone were responsible for permitting the absentee ballot. William Chandler, a New Hampshire Republican, wrote a pamphlet on the soldier vote in which he maintained that the Democrats did not "hesitate to oppose by every means in their power, all attempts to confer upon soldiers in the field the right to vote." They did this, "simply and solely for the reason that they believed the great majority of the soldiers in the army are not for George B. McClellan and the Copperheads but are for Abraham Lincoln, the Constitution, and the Union."[72]

At first, the Radical Republicans in Congress feared that McClellan's personal popularity was so pervasive in the army that as late as January 1863 they had voted in caucus against enfranchising the soldiers for fear they would vote Democratic. Before another year had passed, however, they came to feel that the composition of the army had changed enough to entrust the soldiers with the ballot. General Grant, for one, prohibited canvassing among his troops, but Oswald Villard observed that "no agitation meetings and speeches among the troops in behalf of the candidates of either party was allowed before the election yet so many politicians were serving in the rank and file that considerable quiet canvassing went on nevertheless."[73]

The Election

As Election Day drew closer, charges and countercharges were leveled. Pennsylvania, Indiana, and Ohio held their state elections in October. Sheridan's successful campaign in the Shenandoah Valley was highlighted by his spectacular ride and his army's resounding victory at Winchester, which increased public confidence in the administration. Ten thousand troops were reported to have been rushed home from Sheridan's army to vote in their home states. Yet the soldier vote proved decisive only in a few instances. Of the total vote cast in the field, Lincoln received 121,152 to McClellan's 34,922. In the states where soldiers had to return home to vote, how they voted is more difficult to discern. In Connecticut, where absentee ballots were counted separately, Lincoln won by a scant 2,405 votes. The soldiers cast 2,898 votes for him, thus giving him victory in that state. Out of half a million votes in Pennsylvania, the Union Party won by only about twenty thousand with 26,712 cast by soldiers. In New York, like Connecticut, the soldier vote carried the day, as Lincoln won the state by only 7,740 votes.[74]

Stories from soldiers in camp about election frauds flooded partisan newspapers. False election ballots were distributed through the camps so that they would later be rejected by election officials. On November 1, the *New York Tribune* accused Democrats of digging up unmarked soldiers' graves to secure additional names to place on the ballot list. Officers in camps were accused of opening the envelopes containing soldiers' ballots and destroying Union Party votes. Boxes full of soldiers' envelopes turned up in home states from regiments that had long been out of existence, and the *Tribune* published a list of more than fifty regiments which no longer existed and warned poll watchers to be on their guard. Peace advocates, Copperheads, and draft dodgers who had fled to Canada returned to the United States for brief periods to cast ballots against Lincoln. The *Tribune* believed that the National Union Party had been "cheated" of more than thirty thousand votes.[75]

One soldier wrote that McClellan pamphlets had been distributed in his camp, and since paper was scarce, some soldiers wrapped up their pork ration in the pamphlets. But one member of the 10th Vermont remained loyal to Little Mac and complained about pressure exerted by his officers to vote Republican:

> Camp near Berryville (?)
> Sept. 7th (64)
>
> E Ross Esq.
> Sir
>
> I arrived at the Regt. the 1st of Sept. I found the most of the Boys enjoying very good health except Lewis. He is somewhat unwell just now. We had quite a time last last night waiting for Congressman. I was the only noncommisioned officer that voted the Democratic ticket but we had three majority in our Company. All of our officers are Lincoln men. They would not let Company E vote unless they voted the republican ticket. So there was only 4 votes cast in that Company if I have an opportunity I will vote for little Mac if I have to go to the Rif-Rafs for it. I expect to be redused to ranks for being a McClellanman. But never the less I am going in for the little Mac. I will talk for Him as mutch as I have a mind to. Our Lieut try to make the Boys think that Woodbridge was the only man that was running but I soon learned them better so we came out ahead of them. Three of our Boys have been killed since I was here, I mean three of our Company.
> Please send me some Postage Stamps.
> Yours Truly,
> Edwin R. Buxton[76]

The soldier vote of 1864 has been referred to frequently as the "bayonet vote." That is, the troops voted for the administration, as desired by their superior officers. But the soldier absentee voting laws left no obvious loopholes for fraudulent practices, nor were there clear means to prevent fraud.

The most damaging evidence in support of the "bayonet vote" theory may be found in the case of Indiana, where there was no soldier suffrage leg-

Reelection banner. Ca. 1864. Cloth, 22 × 35 inches. An unusual banner with a bearded image of Lincoln and the date 1860. As Lincoln did not have whiskers at the time of the 1860 election, this was most likely issued for his reelection four years later but carried the date of his original elevation to the presidency. From The Frank and Virginia Williams Collection of Lincolniana; photograph by Virginia Williams.

islation. In this state the crucial election was for the governorship, held on October 11, 1864. A victory for Oliver P. Morton would in all likelihood signal a Lincoln victory in November. Enthusiastic Union Party workers did try to induce soldiers to vote their ticket. Since camp voting was not permitted, soldiers had to cast their ballots within the borders of the state. According to the October 19, 1864, issue of the *Crisis,* a leading Columbus, Ohio, Copperhead newspaper, there was a voting population of six thousand in Indianapolis in 1860, but a gain of four thousand was recorded in the 1864 gubernatorial election. The abrupt swelling of the ballot boxes, according to the Democratic newspapers, was due to two factors. First, members of the 60th Massachusetts Infantry, loyal to the administration, were invited to participate in the Indiana election. Second, according to the *Crisis,* no restrictions were placed on the number of times servicemen could cast their ballots. To support their charges, the Democrats reprinted two letters by members of the Massachusetts regiment that had been published first in the *Boston Courier* and later in the *Quincy (Massachusetts) Patriot.*

One letter, which appeared in the Indianapolis Daily Sentinel on October 31, 1864, read:

> Indianapolis, Ind.
>
> Oct. 13, 1864
>
> Dear Brother: Did you ever attend an election out West? It is a big thing! The people are more enlightened, of course; it is a natural consequence that there is more liberty and freedom than in Massachusetts and benighted lands; so much so that people vote as any times as they please, and allow all their friends to do the same, provided they are "sound on the goose."
>
> It is estimated that the Sixtieth Massachusetts Regiment cast about 6,000 votes for Governor Morton last Tuesday. And I know that some of the boys of Company I voted ten and twelve times each one.
>
> Afterwards, two or three car loads of the regiment were taken to the town of Greenville—about thirty miles from here—and treated to a big dinner. It is a copperhead town (or has been). I think the boys hardly did their duty while there, for the town only gave about 600 Republican majority.

No hard data exist on how sailors voted, because those who did, such as sailors from New York, sent their ballots to their home precincts. Lincoln and Secretary of the Navy Gideon Welles did make special efforts to gather the sailors' votes.[77] Yet duty at sea for long stretches covering the campaign period and the data that do exist suggest that relatively few sailors cast their ballots in the election of 1864.

Likewise, there is no way of knowing precisely how and whether officers voted. A letter written by Gen. George Gordon Meade from his headquarters on November 22, 1864, may indicate what occurred: "I do not know how the fact of my not voting has reached Philadelphia. I cannot help but be flattered that so much importance is attached to my action, particularly as nearly all other general officers, including Grant, did the same — that is, not vote."[78]

Not to be forgotten is the fact that the Army of the Potomac at election time in 1864 was not the same force that George McClellan had commanded and trained in 1861–62. The seven weeks during May and June in 1864 had seen to that. Many of its best and bravest soldiers had been killed or wounded, and thousands of enlistments had expired. Sixty-five thousand Northern boys had been killed or wounded or were missing that spring. This amounted to three-fifths of all combat casualties suffered by the Army of the Potomac during the previous three years. Thus the nucleus of the army that so adored Little Mac no longer existed.

McClellan himself displayed little interest in the actual workings of politics and was intolerant of politicians. Before the Democratic Convention, he wrote to an ally: "Don't send any politicians out here — I'll snub them if they come — confound them!"[79] Although he recognized the necessity of greeting the politically influential during the campaign, he did so no more than necessary. In response to one delegation's request for a meeting, he pleaded: "Can't you invent *some* way of getting me out of the scrape?"[80] He dutifully corresponded with party leaders and campaign organizers, but he preferred writing them to meeting them.

But the single issue of stopping the war short of total victory eroded McClellan's support and bolstered Lincoln's, even among those otherwise disposed to vote against him. One cartoon showed a soldier reacting to McClellan's supposed readiness to end the war and give in to Jefferson Davis: "Goodbye 'little Mac' — if that's your company, Uncle Abe gets my vote."[81]

By October, electioneering in the army camps was unmistakable. Troops raised "Lincoln liberty polls" in their company streets at Petersburg, Virginia. Torchlight parades were staged for both candidates. Despite the stormy prelude, the rainy, dismal Election Day passed quietly. Lincoln went to the War Department at about 7:00 P.M. to follow election returns with his colleagues.[82]

William Ward, wood engraving from *Harper's Weekly.* New York, October 29, 1864. The artist depicts soldiers voting in camp. The first time soldiers were allowed to vote in the field proved a relatively benign, well-organized, and structured affair, with very few occasions of fraud. From The Frank and Virginia Williams Collection of Lincolniana; photograph by Virginia Williams.

When the returns were all in, Lincoln's National Union Party had won a popular majority in twenty-two out of twenty-five states, losing to McClellan only in Kentucky, Delaware, and New Jersey. Lincoln had garnered 55 percent of the popular vote, McClellan 45 percent. The final vote was 2,219,924 for Lincoln and 1,814,220 for McClellan.[83] Senator John Sherman wrote to his brother, General Sherman: "The election of Lincoln scarcely raised a ripple on the surface. It was anticipated."[84] But his letter evidences none of the anxiety he had felt a few weeks earlier when he despaired of Lincoln's reelection.[85]

Conclusion

Soldiers left no doubt that they saw in the election outcome something greater than just vote tallies. A New York sergeant called it "a grand moral victory gained over the combined forces of slavery, disunion, treason, tyranny."[86] A cavalryman who had been deeply attached to McClellan two years earlier now suggested to his father that the results provided proof "overwhelmingly conclusive of the fact that this is a people's war—I thank God that the result is as it is—it is the heaviest blow the rebels have received in a long time."[87]

It was the first time people anywhere, including its soldiers, in the midst of a civil war, ever enjoyed the choice of voting for continuing the war or making peace. Or perhaps it just looked that way, for actually both Lincoln and McClellan favored pursuing the war to victory. But McClellan would have revoked the Emancipation Proclamation in so doing and in reality might not have been able to continue the war if elected. Even more remarkably, the election had involved the soldiers in the field.

Throughout the long campaign months, while the politicians bickered and plotted, Lincoln always kept his vision of nationhood beyond the minor problems of the parties. And the soldiers seemed to recognize this. The presi-

Printmaker unknown, *Union,* second state of the original 1850 engraving by Henry Sadd after a painting by T. H. Matteson. Probably New York, ca. 1860. Several faces from the earlier version were here replaced by those of more current political leaders. Lincoln's head replaced that of John C. Calhoun. His portrait was based on the 1860 Mathew Brady "Cooper Institute" photograph. From The Frank and Virginia Williams Collection of Lincolniana; photograph by Virginia Williams.

dent expressed his faith in his August 26, 1863, letter to James C. Conkling of Springfield:

> The signs look better. The Father of Waters again goes unvexed to the sea. Thanks to the great North-West for it. Nor yet wholly to them. Three hundred miles up, they met New-England, Empire, Key-stone, and Jersey, hewing their way right and left. The Sunny South too, in more colors than one, also lent a hand. On the spot, their part of the history was jotted down in black and white. The job was a great national one; and let none be banned who bore an honorable part in it. And while those who have cleared the great river may well be proud, even that is not all. It is hard to say that anything has been more bravely, and well done, than at Antietam, Murfreesboro, Gettysburg, and on many fields of lesser note. Nor must Uncle Sam's web-feet be forgotten. At all the watery margins they have been present. Not only on the deep sea, the broad bay, and the rapid river, but also up the narrow muddy bayou, and wherever the ground was a little damp, they have been and made their tracks.[88]

The troops shared Lincoln's vision of a new and better civilization and a more democratic nation. They were opening the gates to all. To the soldiers, Lincoln became more than a statesman. He was a prophet and a sculptor of democracy. The troops understood that their sacrifices were being waged for justice, self-government, and progress. Those were the values Lincoln epitomized. Both he and the Union soldiers understood what made the fight worthwhile.

Americans undoubtedly will meet great crises in the future as they have in the past. Superhuman exertion and sacrifice may well be called for again. To those who bear the strain and agony, like their Civil War ancestors, there will echo down the inspiring words Lincoln uttered in 1863: "Thanks to all. For the great republic — for the principle it lives by, and keeps alive — for man's vast future — thanks to all."[89]

Notes

1. Wilson, 1:123.
2. Gibbon, 78–79.
3. *Collected Works*, 5:510.
4. Ibid., 3:27.

5. Nicolay and Hay, 9:364.

6. Ibid., 3:512.

7. Davis, *Lincoln's Men,* 4.

8. Ibid., 23.

9. McCullough, 837–38.

10. Dennett, 35.

11. *Collected Works,* 5:111.

12. Ibid., 119.

13. Ibid., 149, 151.

14. Ibid., 155.

15. Ibid., 182.

16. Ibid., 185.

17. Ibid., 255.

18. Ibid., 273.

19. Sears, 416.

20. Ibid., 427.

21. Dennett, 416.

22. *Collected Works,* 5:426.

23. Ibid., 474.

24. Cullom, 91. Reported by Ozias M. Hatch.

25. Beale, 1:105.

26. Ibid., 1:229.

27. Dixon, 403–4.

28. Welles, *Lincoln and Seward,* 197.

29. Florence Cox, 84–85.

30. J. V. Boucher to Rachael Boucher, n.d. (September 1862), Boucher Family Papers Civil War Miscellaneous Collection, United States Army Military History Institute, Carlisle Barracks, Pennsylvania (hereinafter CWMC, USAMHI). This and all further quotations from the Army of the Potomac soldiers are cited to their original sources, but have been culled for purposes of this paper from the research files gathered by historian William C. Davis, which were generously loaned to the author and used frequently herein with Mr. Davis's kind permission.

31. William E. Dunn to his sister, September 10, 1861, William E. Dunn Papers, *Civil War Times Illustrated* Collection (hereinafter CWTI).

32. Duram, 23, 25.

33. *Collected Works,* 5:485.

34. Emery Edson Doaru, November 11, 1862, CWMC, USAMHI.

35. Nevins, 109–10.

36. George B. McClellan to Mary Ellen McClellan, November 17, 1861, Sears, 135.

37. Dawes, 100.

38. Jonathan W. W. Boynton Memoir, CWMC, USAMHI.

39. Kent, 135.

40. Engert, 28.

41. *Collected Works,* 7:514.

42. Long, 283.

43. *Chicago Tribune,* January 21, 1864.

44. Simon, 12:212–14.

45. McSweeney, 140–41.

46. Edwin Morgan to Edwin McMasters Stanton, September 15, 1864, Stanton Papers, Library of Congress.

47. Henry Kauffman to Katherine Kreitzer, October 15, 1864, in McCordick, 89.

48. Samuel J. Marks to Carrie Powers, October 1, 1864, Samuel J. Marks Papers, CWMC, USAMHI.

49. Drake, 115.

50. Barber and Harland, 626–27.

51. *Collected Works,* 7:512.

52. Noe, 272–73.

53. Sunderland, 147.

54. Long, 280.

55. *Collected Works,* 7:411.

56. Tarbell, *A Reporter for Lincoln,* 70–71.

57. Carter, 480.

58. Athearn, 218.

59. Lamon, 185.

60. Hofstadter, 169.

61. *Collected Works,* 5:530.

62. Hofstadter, 169.

63. McPherson, *Battle Cry of Freedom,* 558.

64. Ellis, 306.

65. Donald, *Lincoln,* 385.

66. Greenleaf, 19.

67. J. V. Boucher to Rachael Boucher, September 29, 1862, Boucher Family Papers, CWMC, USAMHI.

68. Jacob Behm to Jacob Seiler, February 18, 1863, Jacob Behm Papers, CWTI.

69. James Abraham to Mary Abraham, March 5, 1863, Abraham Papers, CWTI.

70. J. V. Boucher to Polly Boucher, January 2, 1863, Boucher Family Papers, CWMC, USAMHI.

71. Long, 285.

72. Chandler, 3–4.

73. Villard, 200.

74. Long, 285.

75. *New York Tribune,* November 17, 1864.

76. Edwin R. Buxton Papers, privately owned.

77. *Collected Works,* 8:43.

78. Meade, 2:244–45.

79. George B. McClellan to William C. Prime, August 10, 1864, Sears, 586.

80. Ibid., 606.

81. Currier and Ives lithograph, *The Political "Siamese" Twins: The Offspring of Chicago Miscegenation,* New York, 1864.

82. Miers, 3:294.

83. Long, 285.

84. John Sherman to William T. Sherman, December 18, 1864, Thorndike, 241.

85. Ibid., 239.

86. Frank Wilberforce to his father, November 11, 1864, McGowan Papers, CWMC, USAMHI.

87. John McGowan to his father, December 29, 1864, McGowan Papers, CWMC, USAMHI.

88. *Collected Works,* 6:409–10.

89. Ibid, 410.

7

The End of Slavery: Lincoln and the Thirteenth Amendment—What Did He Know and When He Did Know It?

L INCOLN'S LEGISLATIVE, military, and rhetorical skills formed a seamless fabric of democratic leadership that cloaked a nation during crisis. The passage of the Thirteenth Amendment may be viewed as the legislative peak of Lincoln's leadership in the same way that the Gettysburg victory was ultimately a part of his military leadership and the Gettysburg Address epitomized his rhetorical skill in articulating his national vision. Moral vision and his willingness to act on it set him apart from politicians of his age.

The legislative victory in the passage of the congressional resolution for the amendment to end slavery is often criticized as a corrupt deal. If it is viewed as a legislative tool to end the war, however, the legislative component takes on a different hue. Our sixteenth president used his sophisticated skills to guarantee his progressive vision for the American polity.

For purposes of analysis, this presentation discusses five issues: (1) Lincoln's leadership, (2) the 1861–64 version of the Thirteenth Amendment, (3) the new mandate for the legislative triumph after the 1864 election, (4) the methods used to obtain the legislative victory, and (5) the passage of the amendment as Lincoln's transforming legislative statement on human bondage.

Leadership and Lincoln

Leadership's best contemporary theorist, James MacGregor Burns, has classified leadership into two broad types: transactional and transforming.[1] Transactional leadership calls for bargaining—you scratch my back, and I'll scratch

From "Abraham Lincoln and the 13th Amendment—What Did He Know and When Did He Know It?" presented at the Ninth Annual Lincoln Colloquium of the Lincoln Home National Historic Site on October 22, 1994.

Henry F. Warren, [Abraham Lincoln]. Washington, March 6, 1865. Photograph, 13 ½ × 10 ⅜ inches. Taken two days after the second inaugural, this is one of the last photographs of the president. From The Frank and Virginia Williams Collection of Lincolniana; photograph by Virginia Williams.

yours. Most leadership falls into that classification. Burns identifies Congress as the epitome of transactional leadership. On the other hand, transforming leaders not only preserve the status quo but also seek political and social change. Lincoln's leadership in the passage of the Thirteenth Amendment suggests his adeptness at both kinds of leadership. The fact that it was wartime legislation related to Lincoln's vision for the nation helps to clarify its importance and casts light on the means that were used to gain its passage.

In our book *Abraham Lincoln: Sources and Style of Leadership*, William Pederson, Vincent Marsala, and I have termed Lincoln's personality as "active-flexible" (or what political scientist James David Barber labels "active-positive"). "Active-flexible" leaders have the inherent ability to negotiate between transactional and transforming behavior. Lincoln took an activist approach to the presidency, a style that Alexander Hamilton would have approved, and he employed Machiavellian means as necessary to achieve his ends. Lincoln regarded the Thirteenth Amendment as his ultimate legislative statement, defining the inherent dignity and moral equality of human beings. He used the necessary transactional means during wartime especially to achieve his vision of an America restored to the founding values of the Declaration of Independence.

Garry Wills expresses the critical national need for the transforming leader as he closes his article "Dishonest Abe" with this admonition:

> What seems lacking in current politicians is not the skills of the operator but the goal toward which those skills should, all the while, be working. . . . Until politicians can supply that sense of mission, their very skills — such as they are — will look cheap and cheapening. It is time to rescue the good name of politics, not by renouncing the dubious means that politicians have always used, but by coming up with ends that make the means worth using.

Did President Lincoln use "dubious means" to help secure passage of the Thirteenth Amendment through the waning days of the Thirty-eighth Congress? If he did, did the ends make the means worth using?

Not much has been written about Lincoln's role in effecting passage of the amendment, and what he and others did continues to generate controversy. Of this, Thaddeus Stevens said, "The greatest measure of the nineteenth century was passed by corruption, aided and abetted by the purest man (the President) in America."[2]

The End of Slavery

While President Lincoln's role had to be paramount, there were many others who played crucial roles, including James Ashley, Samuel Cox, William Henry Seward, and Montgomery Blair. But what was Lincoln's effort? And what did he know of the efforts of others?

The 1861–1864 Reality

In March 1861, an early version of the Thirteenth Amendment was adopted by the House and Senate and sent to the states for ratification. Only Illinois ratified it. It provided that slavery, where it then existed, would not be abolished. The amendment had been accepted by the Republican leadership, including President-elect Abraham Lincoln. It was a final attempt to persuade the South that it need not worry or feel threatened by a Republican president. Compromise died when Fort Sumter was attacked.

During the spring of 1864, a resolution for a new Thirteenth Amendment passed the Senate. It provided that slavery should "not exist within the United States" and empowered Congress to enforce this sanction. On June 15, 1864, the resolution was defeated in the House of Representatives that had ninety-four Republicans, sixty-four Democrats, and twenty-five Unionists from border slave states. The vote was ninety-three in favor, sixty-five against. The required two thirds of those voting would have been 105. Proponents fell twelve votes short. Twenty-five congressmen did not vote at all; only four Democrats voted in favor of the resolutions.[3]

The balance of party power shifted later that year as the number of Democrats in the House went from sixty-four to thirty-five in the November 1864 elections. But the new Congress would not take office until March 1865 and would not meet in session until December. The old Thirty-eighth Congress met in the lame-duck session that ran from December 1864 until March 1865.

The nadir of Lincoln's presidency was mid-1864. The nation had been embroiled in civil war for four years. There was dissent against conscription. Nearly every home in the country was draped in mourning. Many in the North wanted peace at any price. Probably more than a million voters believed in the justice of the Confederate cause or at least did not wish to continue the war.

Lincoln feared losing the election. He was pressured to renege on his public commitment to abolition as a condition for peace negotiations, and some argue that the president almost surrendered abolition. They look to Lincoln's letter drafted on August 17 to a War Democrat, which said, in part, "If Jefferson Davis wishes, . . . to know what I would do if he were to offer peace and re-union, saying nothing about slavery, let him try me."[4]

The Republican National Committee urged Lincoln to send a commissioner to Richmond to make offers of peace "on the sole condition of acknowledging the supremacy of the Constitution." Lincoln initially authorized Henry Raymond to go to Richmond and "propose, on behalf [of] this government, that upon the restoration of the Union and the national authority, the war shall cease at once, all remaining questions to be left for adjustment by peaceful modes."[5]

These arguments ignore too much. On August 25, Lincoln met with Raymond, and the decision was made that he would not go to Richmond. Also, the "let Jefferson Davis try me" letter was never sent. Moreover, William Lloyd Garrison, the most strident abolitionist, maintained it was Lincoln who insisted on the antislavery plank of the 1864 Republican platform by making sure that the party endorsed an antislavery amendment.[6]

The 1864 Mandate

Despite his fear of losing, Lincoln won reelection by a large majority, and in his annual message delivered in December 1864 he implored the lame-duck Congress to pass the resolution. He urged its immediate passage even though the elections had produced a large enough Republican majority to guarantee passage the next year by the Thirty-ninth Congress. Speaking of the sentiment to maintain the Union that was manifested by the election, Lincoln especially addressed the border state Unionists and northern Democrats, some of whom had to be won over if he were to succeed.

Recognizing that he was addressing the same House of Representatives that had previously rejected the antislavery amendment, Lincoln made a nonpartisan appeal: "Without questioning the wisdom or patriotism of those who stood in opposition," said the president, "I venture to recommend the reconsideration and passage of the measure at the present session. Of course the abstract question is not changed; but an intervening election shows, almost certainly, that the next Congress will pass the measure if this does not. Hence there is only a question of *time* as to when the proposed amendment will go to the States for their action. And as it is to so go, at all events, may we not agree that the sooner the better?" He reasoned, "In a great national crisis, like ours, unanimity of action among those seeking a common end is very desirable — almost indispensable. And yet no approach to such unanimity is attainable, unless some deference shall be paid to the will of the majority." Lincoln found comfort in the national election, and he observed that "no candidate for any office whatever, high or low, ventured to seek votes on the avowal that he was in favor of giving up the Union. . . . On the distinct issue of Union or no Union, the politicians have shown their instinctive knowledge that there is no diversity among the people."[7]

Meanwhile, he went to work to get the necessary votes. There were several reasons for this sense of urgency. First, the war continued and Lincoln believed that by constitutionally prohibiting slavery, the rebellion would be undermined. Second, if the border slave states supported the amendment, the morale of the Confederacy might suffer. He told Missouri Democrat James Rollins: "I am very anxious that the war be brought to a close at the earliest possible date. . . . I don't believe this can be accomplished as long as those fellows down South can rely on the border states to help them; but if the members of the border states would unite, at least enough of them to pass the . . . Amendment . . . they would soon see they could not expect much help from that quarter."[8]

Lincoln's frame of mind clearly indicates the importance he attached to the border states. It was in the border states where both races were, according to Lincoln, "living their way into new relations to each other." These were real and daily experiences, not simply abstract and intellectual questions as New Englanders and South Carolinians could afford to see them. Lincoln understood the border states could not be lost militarily or politically. Keeping the border loyal was Lincoln's objective since the start of the war. In fact, unless Lincoln kept the border on his mind, these states (and much else besides) would be lost.[9]

We might understand the undercurrents surrounding the issue of the border states if we could only know what Senator John Henderson of Missouri and other border state men said to Lincoln and each other on the emancipation issue. Whatever it was, it was Senator Henderson who introduced the resolution in early 1864 that made its way into Senator Lyman Trumbull's Judiciary Committee and later emerged as the Thirteenth Amendment. By the time of the final vote on the amendment on January 31, 1865, the border states of Missouri and Maryland had already abolished slavery.

From the border state point of view, many recognized by 1864 that they had erred in not accepting the president's offer of compensated emancipation in 1862. As Representative Rollins of Missouri said to his fellow congressmen during the January 1865 debate: "And, sir, if ever a people made a mistake on earth, it was the men of Kentucky, by whom I was somewhat governed myself, when three years ago they rejected the offer of the President of the United States, who, wiser than we were, seeing the difficulties before us, but seeing the bow of promise set in the sky, and knowing what was to come, proposed to us to sweep the institution of slavery from the border states, offering the assistance of the United States, to aid in compensating the loyal men of those states for their losses in labor and property."[10]

A question rarely asked is why Lincoln did not ask Congress to pass the measure one year before, in 1863, as some of his close associates had advised him.[11] The answer may be found within Garry Wills's definition of leadership. Wills believes "a leader does not just vaguely affect others but takes others towards the object of their joint quest." Lincoln led the people to union and ensured that such union would be devoid of involuntary servitude. To do this, Lincoln had to show compromise and flexibility "appropriate for his kind of leadership."[12] The country was not ready for the amendment in 1863, and Lincoln knew it. Lincoln also knew that his Emancipation Proclamation as a war measure limited to those areas still in rebellion did not have the permanence or legal effect that would be found in a constitutional amendment. He needed the amendment to ratify and expand the import of his proclamation.

The president had a more immediate concern in pressing for the resolution in 1864. Clearly, after his reelection, Lincoln did not want slavery or its perpetuation to be part of any peace negotiations. He wanted to clear the issue from the table as soon as possible. With the passage of a resolution abolishing slavery by the Thirty-eighth Congress, any overture by peace commissioners from the South for the continuation of slavery as a condition of their reentry to the Union would be moot. The leverage would have shifted to Lincoln. Lincoln then would have his way: no slavery and a possible negotiated peace.

Thus, the amendment and the Hampton Roads peace conference on February 3, 1865, three days after the amendment's passage, must be linked. To that end, one needs to recognize a moment when Lincoln was disingenuous during the passage of the amendment. When Democrats and other conservatives began to waver in their support of the measure because they heard that rebel peace commissioners were en route to Washington and they feared that an antislavery amendment would kill any chance for peace, James Ashley, the floor manager of the amendment, sent word to Lincoln to write a message stating that no peace commissioners were on their way. Lincoln complied, knowing full well that the rebel commissioners, though not headed to Washington, were coming to or were already present at nearby Fortress Monroe. As Robert V. Bruce has said, "Lincoln could split hairs as well as rails."[13]

By not waiting for the new Congress to attain passage of the resolution for the Thirteenth Amendment, Lincoln revealed his relentless pursuit of a democratic vision. In so doing, he legitimized the war effort, sent the border states a message, and prevented his transformed goal from being compromised by a peace mission. No ordinary politician, he would act now rather than wait.

The Two-Vote Legislative Victory

Lincoln used every political skill he had to secure passage of the Thirteenth Amendment. His knowledge of Congress and what it would take to pass the measure governed his political thought and action. For example, his hand can be seen in (1) the Nevada statehood issue, (2) patronage, (3) pressure lobbying, and (4) the most controversial and dubious of all—the slush fund. These represent his exercise of transactional leadership in support of moral vision.

Charles A. Dana, assistant secretary of war, claimed that Lincoln expedited the admission of Nevada to the Union in order to have an extra state to ratify the amendment.[14] Earl S. Pomeroy doubted Dana's account—more precisely, he thought that Dana had wedded the enabling bill of Nevada in the spring of 1864 to the passage of the Thirteenth Amendment in January 1865.[15] As Pomeroy indicated, Lincoln would have been in favor of Nevada's admission, regardless of whether that state might help ratify the amendment. It would support his reelection and increase Republican strength in Congress. It is somewhat doubtful he would have been manipulative as early as the spring of 1864 to get the resolution passed. His first public plea for the amendment was not until the summer of 1864. Moreover, the merits of admitting Nevada, for the sake of the amendment, Lincoln's reelection, and the Republican Party, were fairly well known in spring 1864. If Lincoln did press for Nevada's admission, he was not showing much more foresight than others in his place would have shown.[16]

Various sources have Lincoln, or his agents, offering patronage or political favors to persuade reluctant Democrats or border statesmen to vote for the amendment resolution. For example, John B. Alley, a Republican congressman from Lynn, Massachusetts, recollected twenty-three years later:

> Mr. Lincoln was a thorough and most adroit politician as well as statesman, and in politics always adopted the means to the end, fully believing that in vital issues, "success was a duty." In further illustration of this feeling and sentiment, I need only refer to his action and conduct in procuring the passage of the constitutional amendment abolishing slavery. It required a two-thirds vote of Congress to enable the amendment to the Constitution to be sent to the legislatures for ratification, and there were two votes lacking to make two-thirds, which Mr. Lincoln said "must be procured." Two members of the House were sent for, and Mr. Lincoln said that those two must be procured. When asked, "How," he remarked: "I am President of the United States, clothed with immense power. The abolition of slavery by constitutional provision settles the fate, for all coming time, not only of the millions now in bondage, but unborn millions to come a measure of such importance that those two votes must be procured. I leave it to you to determine how it shall be done; but remember that I am President of the United States clothed with great power, and I expect you to procure those votes." These gentlemen understood the significance of the remark. The votes were procured, the constitutional amendment was passed, and slavery was abolished forever. Some, I know, would criticize Mr. Lincoln's methods. But he was a thorough politician, and believed most fully in this case the consequences resulting from his action justified him in resorting to almost any means to procure for that down-trodden race such a boon.[17]

Alley gives the impression that he heard the story from one present when the president purportedly said this. Of all the recollected words of Lincoln by authors who reported what he said, his "I am President of the United States, clothed with immense power" does not sound like the Lincoln we know. It is not included in the Fehrenbachers' *Recollected Words of Abraham Lincoln*.

Albert Gallatin Riddle, an Ohio Republican congressman, recalled twenty-seven years after the amendment that the mission of securing the required two-thirds vote went to a fellow Ohio congressman, James M. Ashley. One Democrat, Representative Anson Herrick, wanted a post for his brother in New York. Another, not named by Riddle, was told that an endorsement for a seat in the next Congress "would depend entirely on his vote." And, although not substantiated, a third lawyer, Andrew J. Rogers, sought to prevent legislation from ending his client's railroad monopoly. Michael Vorenberg has surmised from papers and newspapers that Rogers's abstention was quite purposeful, and it seems to be general knowledge that he was a paid lobbyist for the Camden and Amboy Railroad. Therefore, if anyone was likely to be a party to a Camden-Amboy trade for the Thirteenth Amendment, it was Rogers. But Riddle may have had other wheeling and dealing in mind, and Rogers's absence may have been for some other cause. After all, Riddle's account speaks of a Pennsylvania railroad, not a New Jersey line. For all we know, Jesse Lazear, the abstaining Democrat from Pennsylvania, may have been the Democrat of whom Riddle was writing. In any event, Riddle indicates that the three he mentioned got their wishes.[18]

In their Lincoln biography, John Nicolay and John Hay reported the now-famous incident of lobbyists for the New Jersey railroad offering to buy Democratic votes for the amendment resolution if Lincoln would somehow kill the bill sponsored by Senator Charles Sumner that would have broken the infamous Camden and Amboy monopoly. Historians' efforts to uncover the truth about that allegation have proven fruitless. The important fact is that Lincoln refused to do anything to help the lobbyists. He asserted, "I can do nothing with Mr. Sumner in these matters." Nicolay and Hay give us no more details but say generally that "it is not unlikely" that influences of "selfish interest, operating both for and against the amendment, were not entirely wanting."[19] Yet Sumner's bill to end the railroad monopoly did not pass that session. In fact, it was not reported out of committee. Vorenberg has researched New Jersey archives and ascertained that lobbyists for the railroad were hard at work at the time the amendment resolution was close to passing, so Nicolay's story seems persuasive.[20]

It is unlikely that any deals involving the Camden and Amboy Railroad had much effect on the amendment resolution, although it may be fair to surmise that Andrew J. Rogers, Democratic congressman from New Jersey, abstained from voting on the amendment because of pressure from the railroad lobby. Had he voted, he most certainly would have been against it. According to Vorenberg, it was clear that the railroad was going to fold at the time of the vote, and, in fact, it was bought out in 1866.[21]

Montgomery Blair, who wanted his share of the credit for lobbying Democrats, corroborated the appointment of Herrick's brother as internal revenue assessor in New York. Lincoln personally interceded with Kentucky congressman George Yeaman, who, after voting for the amendment resolution, became minister to Denmark in 1865 — though this may have been a reward for his general loyalty. It has been alleged that Lincoln also offered James Gordon Bennett the coveted post of minister to France for his help in persuading Democrats to support the amendment, but Bennett supported the amendment as early as February 1864, long before Lincoln came out publicly for it.[22] So why did Lincoln need to use any pressure to influence this editor?

For those in favor of the measure, every hostile member who stayed away at voting time aided their attempt at passage. Absence of opponents reduced the number required to constitute two-thirds of those voting. On January 31, 1865, Congressman Andrew J. Rogers and seven other Democrats (Jesse Lazear of Pennsylvania, John F. McKinney and Francis C. Le Blond of Ohio, Daniel W. Voorhees and James F. McDowell of Indiana, George Middleton of New Jersey, and Daniel Marcy of New Hampshire) stayed away. One hundred seventy-five members voted, and the amendment resolution carried 119 to 56 — a margin of two votes above the required two-thirds majority. Democrat Moses Odell from Tarrytown, New York, a lame-duck congressman who represented Manhattan, was appointed navy agent for the city of New York at the end of 1865.[23] It is doubtful that Odell was rewarded specifically for his support of the amendment resolution, since he voted for it in the first session of the Thirty-eighth Congress before Lincoln and Seward started handing out rewards for supporting the measure. He was one of sixteen Democrats who voted for the amendment. Among the others were James E. English of Connecticut, A. H. Coffroth and Archibald McAllister of Pennsylvania, Wells A. Hutchins of Ohio, Augustus C. Baldwin of Michigan, and Anson Herrick, William Radford, Judge Homer A. Nelson, John B. Steele, and John Ganson of New York.[24]

Historian James Rhodes had the assistance of Congressman Ashley's son when he prepared his multivolume *History of the United States from the Compro-*

mise of 1850. On this question, he concluded, "Money could probably have been raised for an attempt to buy up the wavering members, but it is doubtful whether any was used for this purpose." The Democrats, he continued, were "won over through the process of log rolling"—votes on one issue being exchanged for votes on another.[25]

More mysterious is the allegation of Congressman George W. Julian, Indiana Republican, who wrote that success "depended upon certain negotiations, the results of which were not fully assured, and the particulars of which never reached the public."[26] Thaddeus Stevens believed to his dying day that "influence from the White House secured votes against a favorite measure of Mr. Stevens for [a] railway from Washington to New York. These same votes helped Mr. Lincoln's amendment for permanent emancipation."[27]

Lincoln lobbied other Democrats in 1864, too. He appealed to their traditional image as the party of the people by pointing to the huge majority that had voted for Republicans and their platform. After his reelection, the president noted, "It is the voice of the people now, for the first time, heard upon the question."[28]

The Democrats were listening. Having been badly bruised in previous elections, they were perceived as the "pro-slavery party." Samuel "Sunset" Cox argued twenty years later that the Democrats as much as the Republicans deserved credit for passage of the resolution.[29] Cox, whose nickname was bestowed on him by a rival editor for his editorial "A Great Old Sunset," which described a "stormful sunset," did not want to be viewed as favoring slavery.[30] He and others wanted to do what was good for the country, especially in expediting the end of the war. So, according to their memoirs, Cox and other Democratic congressional leaders released their members to vote their consciences.

This is exactly what Lincoln desired—a bipartisan policy. If the Democrats joined in the resolution, it would send a message to the Confederacy, disrupt the more virulent members of the Democratic Party, and show union of purpose.

Did Abraham Lincoln corrupt Democratic congressmen to pass the amendment resolution? Not one of the five reporters—Alley, Stevens, Rhodes, Julian, or Riddle—was actually present. Did they repeat probative hearsay? Were some of them attempting to disparage Lincoln? All of their accounts appeared many years after the events. In addition to prejudice, there could have been a faulty memory and erroneous memorializing of the events and words.[31] For example, the quotation from Stevens, although it sounds like him, is undocumented as to time and place, and the others wrote long after the events, increasing possibilities for bias, errors in memory, and errors in transcription. Many were also referring to a questionable rumor prevalent in February 1865 that Democrats who voted for the amendment or abstained did so because they were bought out by a secret fund, usually given a value of about fifty thousand dollars. Certainly, much money and patronage were being offered for votes. In the words of one lobbyist, "Money will certainly do it, if patriotism fails."[32] Yet the availability of money and political favors does not mean that such offers were accepted. In Sunset Cox's recollection years later, he revealed that he was offered a bribe by a Radical Republican who became upset because he had failed to get his cut after Cox refused the bribe and told his colleagues to vote their conscience.[33]

Cox, who wound up voting against the Thirteenth Amendment, spent the rest of his life trying to explain his decision. His recollection of a bribe may have been contrived, because he made no mention of it in his first book of memoirs (published immediately after the war); also, in 1885 he attempted to revise the pro-slavery image of the Democratic Party to one that was part of a coalition to help end the war.

The relationship of Cox and James English of Connecticut is interesting. Immediately after the amendment passed, Cox's enemies within the Democratic Party—the "Copperhead" peace men—began to circulate stories that he had been responsible for getting some Democrats to vote for the measure, even though he himself had voted against it. That story served the purpose of smearing Cox as being duplicitous, and it quelled rumors that the Democratic bolt on the amendment resolution represented an impending, permanent split in the party. The story was put forward particularly by James Brooks in New York and Alexander Long in Ohio. (Long and Cox had been feuding for a year, and Long contributed significantly to Cox losing his reelection bid in 1864.) According to the tale, Cox urged English to vote for the amendment resolution and promised that he himself would vote for it. English did vote for it, but Cox backed out of the supposed deal. Cox denied the story in a letter to Manton Marble and said he had nothing to do with English's vote. The evidence is inconclusive. Whitelaw Reid reported that English told him that Cox announced his intention to vote for the amendment resolution. But English also had told Reid that he intended to vote for the measure anyway, regardless of what Cox did.[34]

Another piece of the English puzzle lies in the Elihu Washburne Papers in the Library of Congress. In that collection is a letter from Horace Greeley, written just after the amendment resolution passed, telling Washburne that the Republicans should support English's candidacy for governor of Connecticut in 1866. Greeley's decision to back a Democrat may have come independently of English's role in the Thirteenth Amendment, but it may also be a hint that Greeley, and perhaps other Republicans as well, promised English that they would help him in the gubernatorial race if he voted the "right way" on the amendment resolution. This still does not suggest a deal between English and Lincoln. In any case, English was probably not the congressman referred to in Albert Riddle's recollections, because Riddle had his eye not on the next Congress but on the Connecticut governorship.[35]

Mention should also be made of the "Seward lobby" in effecting passage of the amendment resolution. Secretary of State William Henry Seward enlisted the aid of four Democratic operatives—W. N. Bilbo, Emanuel B. Hart, Robert W. Latham, and George O. Jones—to work on New York congressmen for their support. Bilbo found Congressman Homer A. Nelson to be most helpful, and Nelson subsequently voted for the amendment resolution. Nelson was offered a foreign post at the end of his term in March 1865—clearly in appreciation for his support. He declined, asking Seward instead for a position in the Treasury Department. Latham and Seward also had contact with Sunset Cox. On January 12, 1865, Cox created a sensation in the House by arguing that the amendment resolution, while inexpedient, was unquestionably constitutional, thus pulling out from under the Democratic opposition its major argument. At the time it was believed that there were three votes lacking for passage. Cox made it a point to invite Democratic friends to his boardinghouse room and asked them to vote or absent themselves from the vote in order to bring about the "upbuilding of the party . . . to drive this question [slavery] . . . from the political arena."[36] Seward later praised Cox as the man "to whom personally, more than any other member, is due the passage of the Constitutional amendment in Congress abolishing African slavery."[37]

While we know that Lincoln exerted pressure independently of the Seward lobby, especially upon border state members whose support was of great importance, and while other influences were undoubtedly at work to convince wavering Democrats, the number of New York Democrats who voted for the amendment strongly suggest the success of the Seward lobby. Of the sixteen affirmative Democratic votes, six came from New York. The fullest discussion of the Seward lobby is contained in *Politics, Principle, and Prejudice, 1865–1866* by LaWanda Cox and John H. Cox, who have concluded, "That money and patronage were available to speed passage of the Amendment . . . is not merely credible; it is undoubtedly correct."[38]

Cox's change of heart in supporting the amendment—even if *sub silento*—may have come about through such correspondence as that of Kentucky senator James Guthrie, who wrote from Louisville on January 22, 1865: "The proposed Amendment to the United States Constitution had better pass this session than to have a called session and a few months postponement. The agitation in Kentucky will be about the same, and in other states, perhaps less. The interval between March and December next ought to be left to the military arms of the Government."[39] And one can only guess what President Lincoln intended to discuss with Sunset Cox when he invited him for a March 3 meeting at the White House "if he pleases to call."[40]

Whitelaw Reid knew of a fund for swaying congressmen, but he also was convinced that the fund was hardly touched and that it made no real difference.[41] There were political deals of the sort described by LaWanda and John Cox, James G. Randall, and Richard Nelson Current, but it is doubtful that these deals were nearly as important in passing the amendment as were the above-board decisions of War Democrats and border statesmen to take a new stance on the issue of slavery.

It is probable, although not certain, however, that the president did bargain to get swing votes, as patronage was the regular instrument by which Lincoln enticed his Republicans in Congress. Lincoln may have seen no difference between patronage and a trade for a specific vote.

Would a presidential promise to appoint a congressman to a government job violate the bribery statute of 1853?[42] The act prohibited any "bribe, present or reward" or "any other valuable thing whatever" given in exchange for a vote. The 1862 bribery statute, signed by Lincoln, was also broadly drawn to include "any officer of the government" who took money, property, or other valuable consideration for "attention to, services, action, vote, or decision."[43] Would absenting oneself from a vote constitute "services" or "action" or "decision"? Would such a congressman who did such violate the 1862 statute?

The drafters of the Constitution did fear that "the immense power" of the president might lead to corruption. As John Noonan has observed:

> In terms of law as actually enforced, Lincoln's use of presidential patronage was not bribery. . . . If his conduct was to be characterized as corrupt, it would be in terms of a moral standard whose practical enforcement would have been political.
>
> If Lincoln had lived, if the Democratic-controlled House in 1874 had investigated the circumstances of the passage of the Thirteenth Amendment, it is possible that a price may have been exacted in political terms to the detriment of Lincoln's reputation for what was done in January 1865. The investigation did not occur, Lincoln did not live, and his death, overshadowing everything, became a redemptive act sealing the emancipation in a way his use of patronage could never have achieved.[44]

There was no "smoking gun." And besides, Lincoln was too much of a political operative to leave any incriminating memoranda behind.

The Transforming Legislative Act

Whereas other political leaders of his day, both at home and abroad, fixated only on Machiavellian means and ends, Lincoln practiced the pure art of politics within acceptable moral bounds. Lincoln did not have to sign the amendment resolution, but he did so on February 1, 1865, the day after its adoption. Rivers of ink have flowed as experts endeavored to explain why he decided to do this, but room remains for speculation.[45] Lincoln himself expressed satisfaction. "This amendment is a King's cure for all the evils. It winds the whole thing up."[46] Ten weeks later, Lincoln's death legitimized the emancipation and redeemed the slaves already freed by the bargains of congressional politics.

The best way to end slavery permanently was to pass the Thirteenth Amendment while winning the Civil War so that there would be no temptation to backslide. The history of Reconstruction suggests Lincoln's prescience on how to handle equality in America. His leadership made it possible. His death made it more difficult.

Notes

1. Burns, *Leadership,* 4.
2. Scovel, 550.
3. Noonan, 455. Actually this earlier Thirteenth Amendment was ratified by Illinois in 1862.
4. Lincoln to Charles D. Robinson, August 17, 1864, *Collected Works,* 7:501. See also McPherson, *Battle Cry of Freedom,* 770.
5. Lincoln to Henry Raymond, August 24, 1864, *Collected Works,* 7:517.
6. William L. Garrison to Helen Garrison, June 9, 11, 1864, William L. Garrison MSS, Boston Public Library. See also Paludan, 300.
7. Annual Message to Congress, December 6, 1864, *Collected Works,* 8:149.
8. Arnold, 358–59.
9. Phillip Shaw Paludan to author, July 22, 1994.
10. Arnold, 361.
11. Vorenberg, 36–43.
12. Wills, *Certain Trumpets,* 19.
13. Bruce, 14. In an October 27, 1994, telephone conversation with the author, Bruce indicated that he intended to write, "Lincoln could split hairs as well as rails and infinitives," but decided that this would be too humorous.
14. Dana, 174–77.
15. Pomeroy, 362–68.
16. Vorenberg, 180 n. 19.
17. Alley, 575.
18. Riddle, 324–25.
19. Nicolay and Hay, 10:84–85.
20. Vorenberg, 199–202.
21. In a letter to the author dated December 28, 1994, Vorenberg states: "The New Jersey Railroad question is a thorny one. The Camden and Amboy Railroad merged with the New Jersey Railroad in 1867 to form the United New Jersey Railways and Canal Company, which still enjoyed exclusive monopoly rights until 1869 under the original charter of the Camden and Amboy Railroad. By 1865, Horace Greeley was ready to drop his fight against the monopoly and allow the monopoly to expire by its natural terms in 1869. Charles Sumner was not so cooperative. He introduced another antimonopoly bill in December 1865, and Elihu Washburne also introduced one in the House. These legislative efforts against the monopoly continued unsuccessfully a few years, and eventually died before the monopoly expired naturally. The best source is George L. A. Reilley's dissertation, 'The Camden and Amboy Railroad and New Jersey Politics.'"
22. Cox and Cox, 28–29.
23. *Biographical Dictionary of the United States Congress,* 1584.
24. Blaine, 538.
25. Rhodes, 5:50.
26. Julian, 250.
27. Scovel, 550.
28. Annual Message to Congress, December 6, 1864, *Collected Works,* 8:149.

29. Samuel S. Cox, *Union, Disunion, Reunion,* 325–28.

30. Lindsey, 10.

31. Noonan, 457.

32. R. W. Latham to William Henry Seward, January 9, 1865, William Henry Seward MSS, Rush Rhees Seward Library, University of Rochester.

33. Samuel S. Cox, *Union, Disunion, Reunion,* 329.

34. Vorenberg, 243, 196–97, 202–3.

35. Vorenberg to author, December 28, 1994.

36. Samuel S. Cox, *Eight Years in Congress from 1857–1865,* 397.

37. Seward speech, October 31, 1868, in Baker, 5:554.

38. Cox and Cox, 28.

39. James Guthrie to Samuel S. Cox, January 22, 1865, Samuel S. Cox Papers, John Hay Library, Brown University.

40. Lincoln to Cox, March 2, 1865, *Collected Works,* 8:328.

41. Vorenberg to author, December 28, 1994.

42. *U.S. Statutes at Large* 10 (1853): 170–71.

43. *U.S. Statutes at Large* 12 (1862): 577.

44. Noonan, 458.

45. McMurtry, 1.

46. Response to Serenade, February 1, 1865, *Collected Works,* 8:254.

8

Warrior, Communitarian, and Echo: The Leadership of Abraham Lincoln, Winston Churchill, and Franklin D. Roosevelt

ABRAHAM LINCOLN, Winston Churchill, and Franklin D. Roosevelt are three of the political Goliaths of the nineteenth and twentieth centuries. Each led a democratic nation through war, and each articulated for both his constituency and posterity the underlying principles for which his nation fought. Were there any other common factors?

One possible way to approach a comparative view of these modern leaders is to explore them in terms of how one premodern society viewed leadership. According to Robert Bly, the highland Mayans of Guatemala used three categories of progressive ascendancy for adult males: the warrior, the community man, and the echo man. Although the step from boy to warrior was fundamental and celebrated, the warrior was not yet considered mature. The communitarian lived for the community—caring for widows and orphans, using his warrior disciplines to protect them, The "echo" was a man who had transcended a culturally defined role and learned to truly hear his people. He embodied compassion and intuition. The focus of the echo man was less on action than on a philosophical understanding of the community's role in the world and the responsibility of the living to both their ancestral past and future generations.

In a sense, Lincoln, Roosevelt, and Churchill represent modern versions of this Mayan ideal. Each became "the echo" of his era, earning a place in modern history. Perhaps the greatest difference between these three leaders

---

Reprinted with permission of the publisher, The Lincoln Fellowship of Wisconsin, from *Historical Bulletin* 56 (2001). © 2001. The essay was developed from a 1995 presentation at the largest Franklin D. Roosevelt conference ever held in the nation at Louisiana State University in Shreveport.

John Chester Buttre. *Abraham Lincoln*. Published by J. C. Buttre, New York, 1864. Border designed by W. Momberger after a photograph by Mathew Brady. Lithograph in color, 13×17 inches. This handsome print featured vignette portraits representing highlights of the Civil War. From The Frank and Virginia Williams Collection of Lincolniana; photograph by Virginia Williams.

Franklin Delano Roosevelt *(seated, left)* and Winston Churchill *(seated, right)* with Gen. Charles De Gaulle *(standing, right)* and Gen. Henri H. Giraud at Casablanca, January 24, 1943. Photograph, 8½ × 10 inches. From the Imperial War Museum, London. Churchill and Roosevelt tried in vain to bring about a reconciliation between the two rival French leaders. From The Frank and Virginia Williams Collection of Lincolniana; photograph by Virginia Williams.

and those in premodern societies is that modern leadership requires a greater degree of action than contemplation. Yet action alone is not enough.

This study examines these three phases (warrior, community leader, and echo man) in the leadership development of Lincoln, Churchill, and Roosevelt. In many ways, it shows that the Mayan evolution of leadership defines their political legacies and suggests links between the distant past, the present and the future.

The Warrior

As a warrior, Lincoln had the least practical military experience of the three. But he was a fast learner and demonstrated astute appreciation of the role of the warrior in modern warfare. Roosevelt learned the importance of military policy and planning as assistant secretary of the navy during the Woodrow Wilson administration. As president, he assembled a competent staff on whom to rely during World War II. Both Lincoln and FDR grew beyond their warrior stage, whereas Winston Churchill, who had far greater practical experience in military matters, was ultimately restricted by his inflated view of himself as strategist.

Lincoln's early military leadership was minimal. The Black Hawk Indian War offered an opportunity to meet his need for public acceptance. He was elected captain by his men, and he made political contacts. He later deadpanned that his principal enemies had been the mosquitoes.[1] Ironically, his military service worked against his first run for state office, as it left him too little time to politick. He had announced his candidacy for the state legislature before his enlistment, which he extended.[2] His opponents enjoyed ample time to campaign against him, and Lincoln lost. But his military service encouraged him to reenter politics and begin the practice of law.

As a congressman, Lincoln adopted the unpopular stance of opposing the role of the warrior-presidency of James Polk.[3] Lincoln believed in Athenian democracy for the United States rather than a Spartan "military industrial complex" state. In fact, as president, he confounded his critics by coming to understand the political role of the military and the reason that wars are fought and won or lost. He eventually displayed a better understanding of war and politics than did many military leaders.

Lincoln's most decisive uses of presidential power occurred as commander in chief when Congress was not in session: calling for initial troops, instituting the blockade, revoking Gen. John C. Frémont's proclamation of emancipation, suspending in some places the privilege of the writ of habeas corpus, and announcing his own preliminary Emancipation Proclamation.

He intuitively recognized the link between war and politics. Lincoln lacked diplomatic training, but contrary to the opinion of many, he did not ignore issues of international interest and their effect on the United States. His direct involvement, for example, helped defuse the "*Trent* affair," which could have led to war with Great Britain.[4]

He devoted increasing attention to military questions, taking the constitutional role of commander in chief seriously. He assumed an active role in the conduct of the war, both in selecting commanders and in determining strategy. Although he made some mistakes, Lincoln became an excellent military leader, realizing that the war could be won by using the North's numerical superiority to seek out and destroy the enemy army. John Hay, one of Lincoln's private secretaries, wrote to colleague John G. Nicolay on August 7, 1863:

> The Tycoon is in fine whack. I have never seen him more serene & busy. He is managing this war, the draft, foreign relations, and planning a recon-struction of the Union, all at once. . . . There is no man in the country, so wise, so gentle and so firm. I believe the hand of God placed him where he is.[5]

Military leadership by the commander in chief was even more essential for a global war than for a fratricidal war four score years earlier. Franklin Roosevelt was, in a sense, the political offspring of his famous "warrior" cousin, Theodore Roosevelt, who had inspired FDR's political development and molded his worldview. TR's belief in his warrior role, shaped largely by his Southern maternal ancestry, led to his eventual publication of the classic naval study of the War of 1812 and his apparent guilt over his father's eva-sion of military service during the Civil War. Given his earlier influences, the Spanish-American War became a necessity in the development of Theodore Roosevelt. Though the popular image of Theodore Roosevelt as a warrior president is overdrawn, he had a sophisticated appreciation of America's place in the world. Like TR, FDR understood the importance of the role of the United States and its navy in world affairs.

In September 1940, FDR transferred fifty obsolete destroyers to Great Britain in exchange for leases of naval bases. He told the new session of the Seventy-seventh Congress in January 1941 that the United States must become the "arsenal of democracy," a bold assertion in an inherently isola-tionist country.[6] A few days after it assembled, the House received a bill, appropriately numbered 1776, that called for supplying material to Hitler's enemies. Despite the opposition of noninterventionists, this bill was passed in March. The Lend-Lease Act was a virtual declaration of war against the totalitarian powers. The legislation effectively ended American neutrality. Using a Lincoln-like analogy Roosevelt explained, "Suppose my neighbor's home catches fire. . . . If I can take my garden hose and connect it up with his hydrant, I may help him to put out his fire."[7]

As long as the war continued, most of the glimpses Americans caught of their president were Roosevelt as commander in chief, a role he relished.

Roosevelt's long-term objective was a Lincolnesque world order in keeping with his Four Freedoms: freedom of speech and expression, freedom of religion, freedom from want, and freedom from fear.[8]

To Eric Larrabee, author of an excellent study of FDR as *Commander in Chief*, Lincoln was "the ultimate standard in presidential military performance."[9] But he found comparing FDR to Lincoln difficult because their "situations were vastly different." Larrabee asserts that "Lincoln dealt with his commanders seriatim, as one by one he had to recognize their inadequacies and replace them." Larrabee's view ignores Lincoln's trust in his generals in the West who were left alone and in command.[10] While Larrabee indicates that Lincoln "possessed no general staff but had to invent it in his own person," he fails to mention the roles of Henry W. Halleck, who became in actuality the first chief of staff of the army, and Secretary of War Edwin M. Stanton, who handled many of the details of running the war. Larrabee has this image of Lincoln "in the War Department telegraph office—looking into space and forming the words with his lips, as he wrote some of the most thoughtful and concise . . . military instructions"; such a scene, Larrabee notes, "is not one in which Roosevelt can be imagined." Larrabee concludes, "Lincoln was a natural, a born military mind, one of the finest his country has produced."

Roosevelt's foremost concern was securing the speediest possible end of the war at the smallest cost in American lives. But realities forced compromise on FDR, just as they did for Lincoln and Churchill. The extent to which FDR's wartime actions fell short of his long-range goals suggests less a failure of will than a consummate talent for achieving a consensus among his own military commanders, the American people and the allies. In exercising his powers as commander in chief, Roosevelt, like Lincoln and Churchill, operated at the apex of the total war making, production, and diplomatic structures of the nation.

As war leader, FDR was a superb judge of officers. As Larrabee has shown, Roosevelt's greatest contribution to victory was his appointment of men like George Marshall, Ernest King, Dwight Eisenhower, Chester Nimitz, and even Douglas MacArthur. He gave these men enormous responsibility; he kept himself informed about military details; and he usually responded to their advice. Marshall and King ensured that FDR did not neglect the war in the Pacific. They counterbalanced his propensity to be swept up by Churchill's impractical plans. The extraordinary organizational skill and passionate attention to detail of Marshall and Eisenhower complemented FDR's habit of improvising and making sweeping generalizations. Roosevelt's excellent general staff handled the details, whereas Lincoln, lacking such staff, was forced to deal personally with details.

As Larrabee points out:

> Roosevelt was no Lincoln, if one is looking for Lincoln's penetrating grip on what was wrong, say, with Meade's failure to pursue Lee after Gettysburg. Roosevelt did not have to concern himself at that level; he did have a general staff, and one he could rely on; he could get some elements wrong and the general propositions right, as he did at Guadalcanal, the campaign he especially cared about, where he wrongly thought that we had overreached ourselves but rightly saw that the point of it was attrition, wearing the enemy down.

Roosevelt did not have to pressure his field commanders to fight, as did Lincoln. "Roosevelt did not have Lincoln's tactical gift," writes Larrabee, but he exhibited the ability to identify the key issues and prioritize them. Nonetheless, "measured against Lincoln, Roosevelt had a mind of similar strategic capacity, and he put it to work with similar effect."

By the time Germany attacked Great Britain in 1940, Winston Churchill had enjoyed ministerial office on and off for almost fifty years. He entered politics under Queen Victoria and retired as prime minister under Queen Elizabeth II fifty-five years later. Churchill was elected to the House of Commons the year before William McKinley was assassinated in 1901 and was still there in 1964, the year after John F. Kennedy was assassinated. His "finest hour" occurred during World War II, when he rallied the British against Hitler.[11]

In one sense, the highland Mayans offer an insight into Churchill's greatest triumph as well as his most severe limitation. If the warrior is fundamental and still admired, societies recognize there is more to life than the traditional Spartan spirit in democratic states. Churchill's triumphs are fully deserved: victories over political enemies, foreign aggressors, and the childhood parental torments he endured. Fortunately, both Lincoln, in the presence of his "angel" stepmother, and Churchill, in the presence of his nanny, were able to overcome obstacles faced at home. Without those enduring life supports, both democratic leaders may have become instead demonic leaders. Despite the support of these women, each suffered recurrent bouts of depression for the remainder of their lives. In 1940, at the moment of England's and Europe's greatest peril, Churchill at last became prime minister and, in A. J. P. Taylor's simple and eloquent phrase, "the saviour of his country,"[12] a phrase often ascribed to Lincoln in 1865.[13]

On May 13, 1940, Churchill delivered his patriotic "blood, toil, tears, and sweat" speech to the House of Commons: "You ask, What is our aim? I can answer in one word: It is victory, victory at all costs in spite of all terror; victory, however long and hard the road may be."[14] Fifteen days later, when threatened with the prospect of losing a large part of the British army at Dunkirk, he told his cabinet colleagues that the country would "never quit the war whatever happens till Hitler is beat or we cease to be a state."[15] This meant that there would be no compromise with Hitler, rejecting in advance any negotiated peace. For this, Churchill has been universally praised, except by author John Charmley, who faults Churchill for not negotiating with Hitler. Charmley apparently forgets that Hitler had a poor record in keeping his promises.

Churchill was able to overcome Conservative Party reservations as events of the war silenced the opposition. Magnanimous like Lincoln, he did not purge his Conservative opponents. Churchill won the support not only of the Conservatives but also of the Liberal and Labor Parties and the trade unions by including Ernest Bevin in his government. As a result, he established political cohesion and unity and engineered an efficient war machine. He directed the war, aided by the chiefs of staff, while his cabinet concentrated on home and party matters.

Like Churchill, Lincoln could listen to others—even his opponents—as equals. For example, he shrewdly fashioned a good cabinet in which two members excelled—Secretary of State William H. Seward and Secretary of the Treasury Salmon P. Chase. He surrounded himself not with political cronies but with former political rivals who considered themselves his betters. He gathered advice from various quarters, listened, and then made up his mind. Yet Lincoln led his cabinet. "I never knew with what tyrannous authority he rules the Cabinet until now. The most important things he decides & there is no cavil," John Hay wrote approvingly in 1863.[16]

Despite his forceful leadership in other areas, Lincoln rarely submitted legislation to Congress. He deferred to Congress in the framing of such important legislation as the Homestead Act, the Land Grant College Act, the protective tariff, and the national banking laws. He had a Whiggish attitude about the presidency: Less is more. This was the root of his assuming executive powers slowly, almost reluctantly, in the Whig Party tradition.

Lincoln's most active role related to the issue of slavery. While he did defer to Congress in matters of slavery where it had jurisdiction — in the territories and the District of Columbia — he used his power as commander in chief to go after slavery in the seceded states. He used his political influence as president to try to get slavery abolished by state action in the border states. In his 1861 annual message to Congress, he urged the members to adopt the plan for gradual, compensated emancipation in the border states. In 1862, when Congress passed the Second Confiscation Act, Lincoln threatened to veto it until Congress addressed his objection to the provision that those in rebellion would forfeit their property forever in violation of the Constitution's prohibition against bills of attainder. Following his reelection, he used his influence to gain passage of the proposed Thirteenth Amendment abolishing slavery (see chap. 7). Never before had he taken such an active role in securing legislation. But, like Roosevelt and other modern presidents, Lincoln found Congress to be a severe trial. While at times strained, as in his taking the unusual step of giving the Wade-Davis bill a pocket veto, his relations with the legislative branch were never severed. A congressman, frustrated with the president's leadership, admonished him, "This government is on the road to Hell, and you are not a mile from there this minute." To which Lincoln responded, "Yes . . . that is just about the distance from here to the Capitol!"[17]

After the firing on Fort Sumpter, he delayed calling Congress into session, giving himself a free hand for more than two months. When Congress did convene, it had little choice but to ratify Lincoln's actions after the fact. Yet Lincoln believed in the necessity of having Congress confirm his acts.

One of Churchill's private secretaries, John Colville, thought that Churchill "had no conception of the practical difficulties of communication and of administrative arrangements."[18] Yet Churchill was determined not to follow the example set by former prime ministers H. H. Asquith and Lloyd George, who had allowed politics to obfuscate strategy and for generals to do as they pleased. He recognized that the system of administering the war should be centralized without emotion and politics. Hastings Ismay, his chief staff officer, saved Churchill from making the fatal mistake of creating an ad hoc staff composed of the prime minister's cronies. As soon as he became prime minister, Churchill, who was already chairman of the Committee of Military Co-ordination, named himself defense minister.[19]

When the British declared war on September 3, 1939, Neville Chamberlain responded to popular demand by appointing Churchill to his old post at the Admiralty. Churchill's energy was soon felt throughout the cabinet. The Norwegian defeats in April and May 1940 shook public confidence in Chamberlain's leadership, and when the German armies entered the Low Countries on May 10, Chamberlain resigned in favor of Churchill, the one man capable of forging a national coalition government. Parliament gave him a unanimous vote of confidence. This confidence was sustained throughout the war, stimulated by Churchill's faith in ultimate Allied victory and by his dynamic oratory.

Churchill also believed that he was a great strategist, but the evidence is to the contrary. Unlike Lincoln and FDR, Churchill was, in truth, the worst kind of amateur general. From beginning to end of both world wars, Churchill was an adventurer who tried shortcuts and backstairs approaches, sometimes with disastrous results. He had earlier been rightly blamed for the Gallipoli fiasco in 1915. Between 1940 and 1945, his schemes included bringing Turkey into the war and invading Norway. His "Mediterranean strategy" mired the British and the Americans in an endless campaign in Italy and delayed the essential invasion of northern Europe by at least a year. His worst decision may have been the "strategic bombing" offense that destroyed the cities of Germany and killed six hundred thousand civilians without appreciably shortening the war. As A. J. P. Taylor tried to explain it, "He lived for crisis. He profited from crisis. And when crisis did not exist, he strove to invent it."[20]

Yet, to John Keegan, Winston Churchill as war leader is easily compared to Abraham Lincoln.

> Like Lincoln, Churchill remained throughout the war at the seat of government; like Lincoln, he embroiled himself throughout the conflict in the processes of representative democracy; like Lincoln, he never rested in his search for generals who could deliver victory, peremptorily discarding those who failed him; like Lincoln, he clung to no doctrinaire principles of strategy, preferring to trust in a few broad policies that he believed best served the long-term interests of the people and the alliance of states he represented.[21]

The Communitarian Leader

The highland Mayans recognize that people do not live for arms alone. Once the peace has been won or a relative state of security has been established, the quality of community life assumes primary importance. Abraham Lincoln's genius was in recognizing the fundamental nature of America's experiment in self-government, its inherent opportunities through which he was able to fulfill himself, and his willingness to participate in his community to maintain this political heritage for others.

Prior to the presidency, almost all of Lincoln's political life was in state politics, where he accepted the values of the Whig Party in promoting internal improvements for a growing nation. He believed government should help trigger economic development. As a state legislator he was a "big spender" for those purposes which benefited both the community and entrepreneurs.

Retreating from active politics for a short time, he reentered it when America's fundamental values were threatened. His enduring legacy is one of preserving the Union in order to safeguard the American dream for all its people. He used his sense of community to reconcile the values expressed in the Declaration of Independence with the Constitution. The ideal of equal opportunity at the community level was nationalized.

Like Lincoln, FDR's political experience began in state politics. He understood that modern political leaders must act—even when they might not have a clear answer to problems. Rather than accept the Great Depression as inevitable, his political steps at least inspired hope.

Roosevelt was known for his peacetime legislative management, beginning with the ninety-nine-day session of the Seventy-third Congress that began on March 9, 1933. It represented the most daring presidential legislative leadership in American history. Dazed, disaffected, and filled with freshmen who owed their victories to Roosevelt's long coattails, Congress found itself subjected to a carefully timed bombardment of bills. Roosevelt sent a rapid succession of presidential messages, sufficiently spaced to avoid confusion. He followed each message with a bill to implement it. FDR thus dealt with the crisis in agriculture, banking, relief, and a dozen other problems with amazing speed. The fact that Congress was passing a presidential menu of laws was never concealed. Never before had the American government so closely replicated the British system of ministerial leadership.

From his inauguration in 1933 until 1939, the president subordinated questions of foreign policy to his battle for the reforms of the New Deal. During the first session of the Seventy-sixth Congress (January 3–August 5, 1939) FDR labored to secure additional appropriations for housing, to liberalize provisions of the Social Security Act of 1935, and to persuade Congress to amend its neutrality legislation. The last initiative would free him to deal with foreign aggressors in the time-honored way of ad hoc diplomacy.

Although the New Deal may have had many shortcomings, FDR intended it as an experiment to preserve self-government. Even critics today recognize his power to inspire, though they desire to dismantle the legacy of New Deal legislation.

In contrast to Lincoln and FDR, Churchill seems never to have truly recognized the needs of ordinary people in ordinary times when the state was not threatened. As James MacGregor Burns has pointed out, the Labor Party had a social package to offer the British people only after Churchill had gallantly preserved their safety and security during World War II.[22] Even if much of this legislation proved questionable in the long run, it addressed their immediate lives.

Gratitude in politics fails to endure even if it momentarily endears. This truism is borne out by the 1864 and 1944 elections. FDR's reelection was much like Lincoln's. In both instances Americans had to choose their leader during wartime. Both incumbents managed only low pluralities. Yet both are remarkable elections for having occurred at all—a tribute to the leadership of both men.

"The Echo"

Just as there is more to leadership once a society prevails over its predators, there is more to leadership than merely transacting bargains among contending factions in society, as Burns has so eloquently described.[23] As the Mayans recognized, leadership must also incorporate the wisdom of those able to discern the true needs of human beings. The "echo" leadership suggests a psychological dimension that Burns and James Chowning Davies recognize as essential to societal health. The echo leader transcends traditional culture boundaries and sees beyond racial, ethnic, and gender stereotypes. Strikingly, the primitive Mayan culture showed as much sophistication in this dimension as some members of the most advanced postindustrial society demonstrate today.

Churchill's historical echo, no matter how much we honor his achievements, especially his leadership in defending Great Britain against the Nazis, is fainter than the FDR and Lincoln legacies. As Davies pointed out in his comparative view of leadership, Churchill was at heart a traditional conservative primarily interested in defending and preserving England and the British Empire. Even sympathetic admirers acknowledge this. Some even accuse him of being a "racist," but it may be that Churchill was so blinded by the British legacy of colonialism that he failed to see the needs of subalterns. If so, he was not the first English leader with this shortcoming.

Churchill possessed little enthusiasm for women in politics and even for women's suffrage — unlike Lincoln, who at age twenty-nine already advocated the vote for women. Ironically, it was England's first female prime minister, Margaret Thatcher, who looked to Churchill as her party's foremost doctrinaire over other Conservative prime ministers.[24]

While some may cite Churchill's "Iron Curtain" speech as of "echo" quality, even it seems to be wearing thin, for new democracies outgrow their historical chains. Nonetheless, his words suggest the penumbra of the "echo" leader:

> In War: Resolution
> in Defeat: Defiance
> in Victory: Magnanimity
> in Peace: Good Will[25]

These words signal the abstract principles that Churchill recognized as being important to good leadership.

Churchill's essence, in retrospect, is the defiant wartime leader. He said on June 4, 1940, at the time of the Dunkirk evaluation:

> We shall not flag or fail. We shall go on to the end. . . . We shall fight on the seas and oceans, we shall fight . . . in the air, . . . we shall fight in the fields and in the streets, we shall fight in the hills; we shall never surrender.

Always the fighter, Churchill did not quite comprehend the needs of the English *after* World War II or the non-English-speaking peoples of the world.[26] He patronized people of Third World countries. In a sense, he revered England as a nation-state and valued the Empire and the English language far more than foreign tongues and peoples.

In strong contrast, Roosevelt's imprint continues to strike a resounding echo today. For example, in the latest rating poll of presidents by American scholars, FDR supplanted George Washington in the number two spot.[27] Though the legacy of the New Deal may be mixed and may have tentacles reaching far beyond FDR's intent, his leadership inspiration remains intact even among some Republicans. Roosevelt's "Four Freedoms" remain a national and even international statement of human rights. They are the ideals of an echo leader.

Although his inner reserve, like that of Lincoln, often baffled even those closest to him, FDR's basic character was in accord with that of many Americans: idealism tempered by realism. He seldom talked about his thinking or his plans until he had firmly made up his mind. According to Larrabee, John Gunther once asked Eleanor Roosevelt, "Just how does the president think?" She responded, "My dear Mr. Gunther, the President never thinks! He decides."[28] On the other hand, Edward J. Flynn writes, "Roosevelt would adopt ideas only if he agreed with them. If he disagreed, he simply did nothing."[29] By not sharing his thought processes, FDR fostered an aura of mystery and authority, and he kept power firmly within his domain. These same characteristics also describe Lincoln.

FDR understood the needs of others. Moreover, he enjoyed the counsel of a First Lady who perpetually educated him about people from less privileged backgrounds. He viewed his wife as his political partner and encouraged her to mold a twentieth-century role for herself. FDR appointed her to his cabinet. He not only could hear the voice of those very different from him; he could also speak their language, as he demonstrated in his Fireside Chats.

While FDR is highly ranked, Abraham Lincoln consistently polls first. His warrior career probably was inspired by George Washington, America's quintessential echo leader. Yet Lincoln did not enter the pantheon as a war hero.

Lincoln was the communitarian leader who recognized the needs of his constituents on the frontier. His legislative career was a model of using government to help people achieve economic advancement. Yet even in this traditional Whig view of internal improvements, Lincoln was sensitive toward others, including politically disenfranchised slaves and women. When his principled position on slavery and the Union thrust him into a wartime presidency, his message was compassionate, a valid echo for all time:

> We are not enemies, but friends. . . . Though passion may have strained, it must not break our bonds of affection. The mystic chords of memory, stretching from every battle-field and patriot grave, to every living heart and hearthstone, all over this broad land, will yet swell the chorus of the Union, when again touched, as surely they will be, by the better angels of our nature.[30]

Similarly, Lincoln's Gettysburg Address exemplifies a genuine echo leader. He speaks of the debt to forefathers, to the living and to the soldiers who have just died, while poetically bringing the Declaration of Independence and the U.S. Constitution into sync for the benefit of all.[31]

Seemingly, it was the genius of Lincoln to understand the needs of everyone all the time. He comprehended the values of our founders expressed in both the Declaration of Independence—"our jewel of liberty"—and the inherent restraints required by the Constitution. Maneuvering between idealistic values while preserving the constitutional restraints imposed on him, Lincoln led the nation during a divisive civil war that ultimately ensured greater human dignity for all. Amazingly, Lincoln accomplished his enduring legacy in one-third the time FDR spent in office and half the time Churchill led wartime Britain. Lincoln's leadership is the modern epitome of classical magnanimity.

Conclusion

In a comparative sense, Abraham Lincoln's leadership remains the touchstone echo. As James C. Davies long ago suggested, Lincoln's democratic example and American federalism are the two greatest gifts that our ambitious experiment in self-government has given the world.[32] Though more conservative than Churchill in many ways, Lincoln was able to expand democratic values whereas Churchill was tied to preserving the British Empire.

Similarly, FDR was able to adjust to an evolving world better than Churchill. FDR was willing to experiment, but he retained his ability to listen to others, including Eleanor, his social conscience. Despite their inherent differences, Lincoln, FDR, and Churchill remain fundamentally effective role models for democratic leaders.

Perhaps the reason that Churchill's leadership echo may resonate less vibrantly than Lincoln's or FDR's is that, without question, he endured the most psychologically stressful upbringing of the trio. He was virtually ignored by parents who favored his brother. Fortunately, as Lincoln found warmth from his stepmother, Churchill found support from his nanny. Both suffered bouts of depression throughout their lives. Churchill's fight for psychological survival may explain his lack of sensitivity toward others. He was the life-long fighter.

In contrast, FDR was afforded the psychological luxury of a secure childhood that allowed him to focus concern on others. Similarly, Lincoln gained psychological security, despite tension with his father, from having to fight for survival on the frontier.

A comparative study of these three democratic giants of the nineteenth and twentieth centuries helps to clarify — and confirm — the significance of each. It also suggests the difference between the ephemeral and the eternal in political leadership, and it calls to mind F. W. Maitland's rule: Events now long in the past were once in the future, and we should interpret these events in terms of how people expect them to turn out, rather than how they do.[33]

Notes

1. *Collected Works,* 2:510.
2. Ibid., 5:511.
3. Ibid., 1:420–22. Congressman Lincoln asks President Polk in his "Spot" Resolutions in the House of Representatives on December 22, 1847, to show exactly the "spot" where Mexico invaded "our territory."
4. McPherson, *Battle Cry of Freedom,* 391. The president was aware that the action of Capt. Charles Wilkes, in halting the mail steamer Trent near the Bahamas and seizing Confederate emissaries Mason and Slidell, violated international law. The commissioners were released after Great Britain threatened war and embargoed all shipments of saltpeter, which the North needed for gunpowder. As the president said, "One war at a time."
5. Dennett, 76.
6. For a full discussion of the FDR's machinations, see Shogan.
7. Frank Freidel, *Franklin D. Roosevelt: A Rendezvous with Destiny,* 360.
8. Ibid., 361.

9. All quotations from Larrabee in this section are taken from *Commander in Chief,* 643.

10. Historian Richard McMurry believes the war was won by the North in the West. See interview with Zebrowski, 26, 66.

11. Taken from a speech delivered by Winston Churchill on June 18, 1940, the day after the French capitulated: "Let us therefore brace ourselves to our duties, and so bear ourselves that, if the British Empire and its Commonwealth last for a thousand years, men will still say: 'This was their finest hour.'" See Churchill, 2:198–99.

12. Taylor, *The War Lords,* 98.

13. See the excellent survey in Peterson, particularly "Apotheosis," 26–27.

14. Gilbert, 333.

15. Ibid., 407.

16. Dennett, 76.

17. Zall, 35, entry 48.

18. Colville, 126.

19. Keegan, 329.

20. Taylor, "The Statesman," 58.

21. Keegan, 330–31.

22. Goodwin, 219.

23. Burns, *Leadership,* 4.

24. Grigg, 111.

25. Inscribed on a statue of Winston Churchill at Westminster College, Fulton, Missouri, site of the Winston Churchill Memorial Library.

26. Davies, 306.

27. Murray and Blessing, 535, 555; Schlesinger, "The Ultimate Approval Rating," 46–51.

28. Larrabee, 644.

29. Flynn, 214.

30. *Collected Works,* 4:271.

31. Ibid., 7:17–22.

32. Davies, 320.

33. Schuyler, 74–75.

9

Lincoln Collecting: What's Left?

Written with Mark E. Neely Jr.

A s the world's greatest democratic political leader, Lincoln invites modern enthusiasts to approach him through a variety of doors. Most Lincoln enthusiasts can trace their interest to a book or some historical document, item, or experience that opened a door for them to Lincoln's enduring legacy and cast a major impact on them. If not a book, perhaps it was a Lincoln coin collection, stamp collection, photograph, or print. For most people these doors have served to reinforce an interest in America's sixteenth president. For others it has led to a life of collecting, sometimes illuminated by scholarship. In turn, these growing passions have sometimes led from individual efforts to institutional legacies as collections are turned over to institutions to further spread the Lincoln message.

The purpose of this essay is to survey the development of Lincoln collecting. The survey suggests the original inspirations of the collector, the tendency of scholars to separate themselves from collectors even though the two pursuits overlap and are indeed dependent on one another, as well the emergence of the investor-collector, whose efforts may work against the motives of both the amateur collector and the professional historian. Despite

Reprinted with permission of the publisher from "Collecting Lincoln: What's Left to Collect" in a 1986 issue of *Manuscripts*. First delivered at Brown University at the symposium "Lincoln and the American Political Tradition" held June 9, 1984, to commemorate the 175th anniversary of Abraham Lincoln's birth, this essay was written with historian Mark E. Neely Jr. and focuses on collecting concrete Lincolniana. This article is also based on a paper delivered at Ford's Theatre, Washington, D.C., on April 13, 1985, as part of a conference sponsored by the National Park Service and the libraries of Brown University. "The Crises in Lincoln Collecting" appeared in the special Lincoln issue of *Books at Brown*, published in 1985 by the Friends of the Library, Brown University.

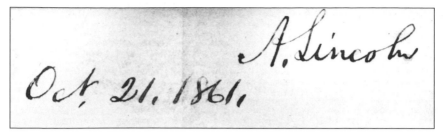

Abraham Lincoln, clipped signature. October 21, 1861. Initially, collectors believed that clipped signatures from full documents were more valuable than the documents themselves. This is my first Lincoln signature, purchased for two hundred dollars in 1972. Today, similar Lincoln signatures sell for five thousand dollars or more. From The Frank and Virginia Williams Collection of Lincolniana; photograph by Claire White-Peterson, Mystic Seaport Museum.

these tensions within the field of collecting, a number of suggestive areas remain open to the amateur who wants to build a professional collection of note.

The Origins of Lincoln Collecting

Collectors like to touch and perhaps relate to ever-changing political phenomena by grabbing a concrete part of it. The first Lincoln collector was a man from Philadelphia named Schlater. We know of him only because Lincoln wrote him a letter in 1849, when Lincoln was an unimportant first-term congressman grown unhappy with Washington life and fast losing interest in politics altogether:

> Dear Sir:
>   Your note, requesting my "signature with a sentiment" was received, and should have been answered long since, but that it was mislaid. I am not a very sentimental man; and the best sentiment I can think of is, that if you collect the signatures of all persons who are no less distinguished than I, you will have a very undistinguishing mass of names.
>
> > Very respectfully,
> > A. Lincoln

More than likely, Schlater had written similar letters to every member of Congress and encountered Lincoln's name as only one of many on a list. But he goes down in history as the first person we know of who collected Lincoln's autograph.

In contrast to Schlater, Lincoln himself never had the impulse to collect. His law partner, William H. Herndon, said of Lincoln, "He had, aside from his law books and the few gilded volumes that ornamented the center table in his parlor at home, comparatively no library. He never seemed to care to own or collect books." Lincoln was an individual of political action.

As his stature in American politics grew, so, too, did his willingness to satisfy the collector's urge. At some level the leader recognized the need of followers, just as the followers recognized a true leader. By the time of his nomination to the presidency in 1860, Lincoln answered collectors' requests in a suave manner. To Edwin A. Palmer, for example, Lincoln wrote:

Dear Sir:
    You request an autograph, and here it is.

                Yours truly,
                A. Lincoln

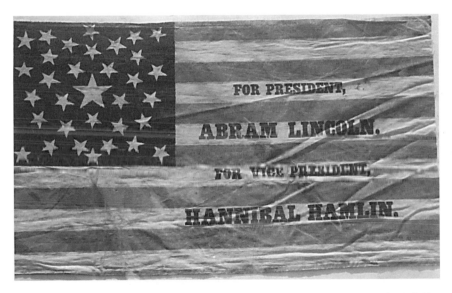

Flag. Ca. 1860. Treated cloth, 10½ × 16¾ inches. A thirty-star flag promoting "Abram" Lincoln for president and Hannibal Hamlin for vice president, this rare textile was probably hoisted in campaign parades. From The Frank and Virginia Williams Collection of Lincolniana; photograph by Virginia Williams.

In the beginning, Lincoln collecting and Lincoln scholarship were inseparable. Most of the early Lincoln bookmen—Daniel Fish, Joseph Benjamin Oakleaf, William H. Lambert, Judd Stewart, and Charles W. McLellan—were collectors. Many of the early biographers and historians amassed substantial Lincoln collections: John G. Nicolay, Ida M. Tarbell, and William E. Barton, for example. Research libraries were so few that an author almost of necessity had to own large numbers of books. There were collectors who did not write and writers who did not collect, but the cross-fertilization was substantial.

A Bifurcation in Lincolniana

Within a half century of Lincoln's death, a great divide had taken place in the world of Lincolniana, however. The professionalism of the writing of history led to a separation between scholarship and collecting, and in the process the heart became separated from the head. The event symbolic of this great divide was the Minor Affair of 1928, when the *Atlantic Monthly* published, on the representations of the charming and attractive Wilma Frances Minor, some ludicrously flimsy forgeries of alleged love letters between Abraham Lincoln and Ann Rutledge. Amateur historians, like Carl Sandburg, and even more importantly, the *Atlantic Monthly* itself, a very high-brow, popular magazine, initially fell for the forgeries. At the same time, professionals like Paul Angle, who was working then for what became today's Abraham Lincoln Association, denounced them.

Finally, in 1936, the professionals issued an official declaration of war. James G. Randall, who would become the greatest Lincoln biographer with his four-volume *Lincoln the President,* was a professional historian in the newest sense. He had a Ph.D. in history, he taught at a university, and he had published a monograph on Lincoln and the Constitution. His paper "Has the Lincoln Theme Been Exhausted?" declared war on the collector and reserved Lincoln scholarship for the college professors. Historians in the Lincoln field are forever quoting his paper to show that it is all right to keep writing on Lincoln and add another Lincoln title to the pile, but they do not quote what was really the main thrust of Randall's argument. He said in the very first paragraph:

The hand of the amateur has rested heavily upon Lincoln studies. And not only of the amateur historian, but of the collector, the manuscript dealer, the propagandist, the political enthusiast, the literary adventurer.

Randall put the Lincoln collector in pretty undistinguished company. By and large, he and his academic colleagues succeeded. Collecting became more and more divorced from advanced scholarship.

Entrance of the Investor

When Randall slammed the door shut on the amateur collector, he opened one for capitalists. Collecting became increasingly enmeshed in the cash nexus. After 1940, it came to be regarded more as an investment than as a scholarly, literary, or cultural pursuit.

And so it has remained — for some — for half a century. In May 1984, publisher Malcolm Forbes paid $231,000, the largest sum ever paid for a Lincoln document up to that time. After that, the *New York Times* quoted him as saying, "I think it's a bargain." And maybe it was, but the fact of the matter is that the article on sale included only the scantiest analysis of the historical significance of the document, the manuscript of Lincoln's last speech. In truth, the speech provided the best clues to what Lincoln would have done had he survived into the period we now call Reconstruction. It was the president's first public announcement of support for Negro voting rights. "It's a better portrait of Lincoln than any other document or painting," Forbes told the press, but the reporters did little to explain why in the newspapers.[1]

The Forbes record was quickly broken — by himself. In October 1984, he engaged in a bidding war at a Sotheby Parke Bernet auction with H. Ross Perot. Forbes, the publishing magnate, and Perot, who apparently developed his interest in Americana more recently, locked into a titanic struggle over an inconsequential document — one of forty-eight souvenir copies of the Emancipation Proclamation sold for charity at the Philadelphia Sanitary Fair in 1864. The documents were autographed by Lincoln and Secretary of State Seward, but their text was printed and they were hardly unique. In the end, Forbes won the document for $297,000, the most money ever paid at auction for a presidential document. Once again he declared it "a bargain," and once again the press said little about its historical significance — this time for good reason.[2]

As a result of this emphasis on price, there are some items that are no longer within the individual and institutional collectors' economic reach, nor are they available at any price. There probably are no more significant documents to be found not already in *The Collected Works of Abraham Lincoln*—no Gettysburg Addresses or unknown speeches on Reconstruction in Lincoln's hand. Those documents which do remain in the private sector will be costly.

Another problem lies in collecting the early books and pamphlets listed in the standard *Lincoln Bibliography* by Jay Monaghan. Monaghan attempted to list in chronological order all the Lincoln items published between 1839 and 1939. Although out of date and not all-inclusive, Monaghan's two-volume set continues to be used by Lincoln collectors and bibliophiles to this day. If we take, for example, the period from 1839, when his bibliography begins, through 1865, we find 834 items listed. The Lincoln Museum, formerly the Louis A. Warren Lincoln Library and Museum, in Fort Wayne, Indiana, is lacking 20 percent of these. This institution bought the Daniel Fish collection in 1930, Mr. Fish being one of the "Big Five" Lincoln collectors who had been collecting for approximately thirty-five years. Since purchasing it, the Lincoln Museum has been avidly collecting for an additional fifty-five years. In ninety years of collecting, this Library still lacks close to 20 percent of the items listed by Monaghan. The McLellan Lincoln Collection at Brown University, building on the collection of another of the Big Five, Charles W. McLellan, is missing 10 percent of the total of 834. The Frank and Virginia Williams Collection of Lincolniana—taking a present private collection as an example—lacks 30 percent of these items. To compound the troubles of collectors further, one need only look at the recent prices realized in the lists of various auction houses. A Lincoln campaign flag sold for seventy-five hundred dollars in 1984. An autographed photograph of Lincoln sold for fourteen thousand dollars in October 1984, then the highest price ever paid for such an item—until March 27, 1985, when Malcolm Forbes purchased an autographed photograph for $104,500.

The New Specialist in Collecting

What, then, is the new collector to do? You could start now and collect everything. Buy every single Lincoln item in print. Check every used and rare bookstore. You might think that you were doing nothing for the scholar or your legacy, because you believe the major libraries contain all that is published. Not so. For example, not all research libraries get the annual *Journal of the Abraham Lincoln Association* (formerly the *Papers of the Abraham Lincoln Association*). It cannot be found in the Princeton or Yale Libraries or in the New York Public Library. The Yale Library asked the Lincoln Museum not to send the annual R. Gerald McMurtry Lectures, which it distributes *free* to all libraries, apparently because cataloging pamphlets is costly.

You may wish to approach collecting Lincoln thematically. Choose one area in which to concentrate, but be innovative and look to coming events. Note that 1987 was the bicentennial of the Constitution. Why not collect, then, items related to Lincoln and the Constitution? These are plentiful and reasonably priced, and the public and the press are soon to become quite interested in them. From the first, Lincoln was beset by issues relating to the Constitution. He suspended the privilege of the writ of habeas corpus in parts of the North shortly after his inauguration. The writ permits one who is detained or arrested to have a court review his incarceration. When the privilege is suspended, there is no such review, and arbitrary arrests are permitted. A Confederate sympathizer, John Merryman, was arrested in Maryland and thrown into Fort McHenry. Chief Justice Roger B. Taney wrote a decision in favor of Merryman, stating that the president did not have the power to suspend the writ. The president ignored the order to release Merryman, arguing that the Constitution permitted him, especially when Congress was not in session, to suspend the privilege "in cases of rebellion and insurrection." While the Constitution permitted suspension, it was unclear who had the power—the president or the Congress. The ambiguity brought forth, as one may expect, a torrent of words from lawyers. An advocate of the president's position was one Horace Binney, who wrote his famous pamphlet in support of the president. It provoked over forty replies in opposition, which, in turn, caused Binney to write two rebuttals. Many of these may be purchased for as little as $10 each.

Most of the famous—and "collectible"—personalities in the Lincoln administration were at one time or another involved with arbitrary arrests. William H. Seward was charged, as secretary of state, with enforcing the arrest of disloyal persons until jurisdiction for these arrests was transferred to the War Department under tough Edwin M. Stanton in 1862.

These arrests were, of course, controversial—none more so than that of

W. J. Baker, [Secretary Seward's Diplomatic Party, at Trenton High Falls, New York]. Ca. 1863.
Carte-de-visite, 4×2½ inches. A rare photograph of the secretary of state with foreign minis-
ters. Seward is on the right. The person standing third from left who looks amazingly like the
photographer Mathew Brady is actually M. Bertenatti, the Italian minister to Washington.
From The Frank and Virginia Williams Collection of Lincolniana; photograph by Claire
White-Peterson, Mystic Seaport Museum.

Clement L. Vallandigham, the most ardent opponent of Lincoln's administration. From jail, Vallandigham wrote that the Lincoln administration would
not hold elections in 1864. This letter cost only $325 in 1980. The issue of con-
scription or the draft, our first national draft, brought forth in addition to
riots, much criticism of the administration. Among the Lincoln manuscripts
still available for a reasonable price ($1,000 to $2,750) is a discharge of a prisoner. There were lots of prisoners, and Lincoln wrote many of these notes.
Likewise, material on the issue of the constitutionality of the emancipation
of slaves is readily available. For example, the pamphlet by William Whiting,
solicitor of the War Department, argued that the president had the right
under the war powers of the Constitution to emancipate the slaves. It is said
that his arguments impressed Lincoln and helped him reach a decision to
issue the Emancipation Proclamation. The Emancipation Proclamation itself
was printed in many forms, becoming a popular item to collect. Charles Eber-

stadt, the bibliographer of the printings of the Emancipation Proclamation, lists fifty-two printings.

One may be led by this theme to collect items about Attorney-General Edward Bates, even though Lincoln was really the lawyer of his administration. The formation and activities of Copperhead groups such as the Knights of the Golden Circle and the Sons of Liberty may also be of interest.

Another likely specialization for the fledgling collector would be the political culture of Lincoln's era. Increasingly, historians have felt that the political system of Lincoln's day was dramatically unlike our own. We recommend collecting items which document that now lost political world. The major differences between the two eras were that politics were vastly more important in Americans' daily lives and politics were more partisan. In an age with no cinema or television, spectacle was an important drawing card. Republican "Wide-Awakes" were especially colorful, dressed in oilcloth capes and caps, carrying torches on rails, and marching with semimilitary precision in night parades. This was not just the rah rah stuff of football, although their floats were highly reminiscent of something like the Rose Bowl Parade.

The paper ballots of Lincoln's day were not secret ballots by any means. Voters picked up their ballots at one of the sheds temporarily placed by each party outside the polling place, carried a paper ballot printed by his party inside and deposited it in one of two clear glass bowls. Well, how about collecting the ballots themselves? Many still exist today. They vary in size, shape, color, and symbolic devices. The result of all of this was a public display of partisanship and enthusiasm for politics unequalled today. National voter turnout in 1860 was a mind-boggling 82 percent. People decorated their homes with political prints. If you asked to see the family photograph album, it might begin with pictures of party heroes and *then* show the family's pictures. The faces of politicians were used like those of sports and entertainment figures today to sell products.

The result for modern collectors was the introduction of a range of now collectible political materials that have no precise modern counterparts. Probably no one now can sing a campaign song from a recent presidential campaign. Some may remember "Hello, Lyndon," and all Democrats think of "Happy Days Are Here Again." But can you remember the "Gerald Ford Polka" or the "Richard Nixon Quick Step" or the "Walter Mondale Schottisch"? Of course not. But in the nineteenth century, there were Stephen Douglas polkas and Lincoln quick steps and McClellan schottisches

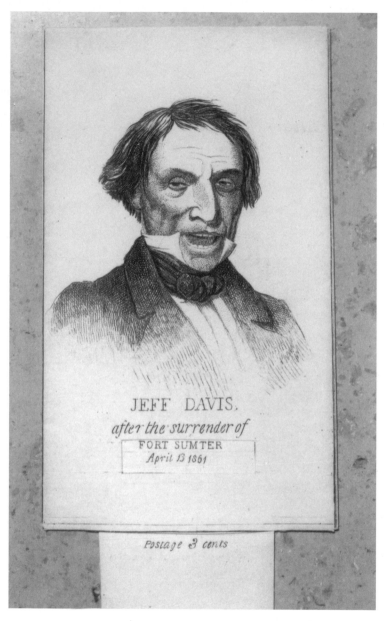

JEFF DAVIS,
after the surrender of
FORT SUMTER
April 13 1861

Postage 3 cents

D. C. Johnston, *Jeff Davis after the surrender of Fort Sumter, April 13, 1861* and *Jeff Davis after the fall of Vicksburg, July 4, 1863*. Boston, ca. 1863. Lithograph, 2½×4½ inches. The pull tab at the bottom of this amusing artifact alters the expression on Davis's face from a smile to a scowl when the printed legend on the tab changes the date from 1861 to 1863. From The Frank and Virginia Williams Collection of Lincolniana; photographs by Virginia Williams.

JEFF DAVIS,
after the surrender of

VICKSBURG
July 4 1863

Postage 3 cents

Campaign badge, bearded ferrotype portrait of Lincoln, which is a reverse profile of the February 9, 1864, Brady photograph, with cloth flag and tin eagle. Ca. 1864, 2½ inches long. Brady's photographs were frequently adopted—usually without permission—for campaign ephemera. This is one notable example of that phenomenon. From The Frank and Virginia Williams Collection of Lincolniana; photograph by Virginia Williams.

published as sheet music with attractive lithographed covers. There were songsheets and songsters, too.

What else is there to collect that documents lost political culture?

Of course, there are campaign biographies (previously unknown satirical ones for Lincoln and Douglas in 1860 sold in 1984 in Chicago for about one thousand dollars each), political prints, posters, advertisements of rallies and speeches, cartoons, campaign newspapers (a McClellan/Pendleton campaign poster was sold in 2000 for about two thousand dollars), photographs of "Wide-Awakes" (one was bought for $225 in 1978), and political envelopes — all of which will help document the lost political world of Abraham Lincoln.

Additional themes for consideration include Lincoln's cabinet or foreign relations. Much has also been written about Lincoln humor — the most recent being the excellent *Abraham Lincoln Laughing* by P. M. Zall.

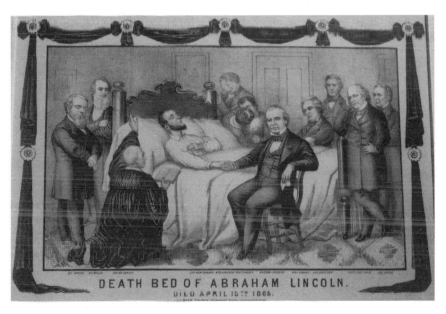

John L. Magee, *Death Bed of Abraham Lincoln/Died April 15th, 1865*. Philadelphia, 1865. Lithograph, 14×9¼ inches. The bizarre "last moments" scene features a diminutive Secretary of War Edwin M. Stanton on the left, the dying president inexplicably holding hands with Vice President Andrew Johnson, and Mrs. Lincoln in the arms of her son Robert, incestuously kissing. From The Frank and Virginia Williams Collection of Lincolniana; photograph by Virginia Williams.

IN MEMORY OF ABRAHAM LINCOLN.
THE REWARD OF THE JUST.

D. T. Wiest, *In Memory of Abraham Lincoln—The Reward of the Just.* Published by William Smith, Philadelphia, 1865. Lithograph, 18¾×24 inches. After Lincoln's sudden and horrific death, printmakers rushed to produce prints for a demanding public. In this apotheosis print, Lincoln's head is substituted for that of George Washington to update an earlier image by John James Barralet, *Apotheosis of George Washington,* published in 1802. From The Frank and Virginia Williams Collection of Lincolniana; photograph by Virginia Williams.

Gabor S. Boritt's *Lincoln and the Economics of the American Dream* might invoke a search for material on banking, internal improvements, the initiation of the use of "Greenbacks," and, of course, Lincoln's ambitious secretary of the Treasury, Salmon P. Chase, who wrote long letters — still available with good content but difficult to read.

One can still collect items relating to Lincoln and the law, his life in Springfield, and his political opponents, such as Peter Cartwright and Stephen A. Douglas. Material on Mary Todd Lincoln is available, including manuscripts. While they are increasing in price, the content remains the same — gossip and her requests for money. The death of Lincoln continues to produce a plethora of material — the making of the legend, the funeral, and the interment. The assassination itself constitutes a major area of Lincoln collecting.

There are many other themes worthy of focus for the aspiring Lincoln collector who is not a millionaire."[3] More important, there is really no reason not to return to the old spirit of Lincoln collecting. An individual collector can hope to accumulate enough to constitute a genuine scholarly legacy. And it would be better for collectors and professors alike if Lincoln collecting turned its back on the notion of investment in historical materials and embraced the more enduring values of scholarship and culture.

Notes

1. On March 27, 2002, the speech was sold at Christie's for $3,086,000.

2. At the same sale of the Forbes Collection of American Historical Documents on March 27, 2002, this manuscript document sold for $721,000.

3. For a current survey of many Abraham Lincoln collectibles, see Stuart L. Schneider, *Collecting Lincoln* (Atglen, Pa.: Schiffer, 1997).

Epilogue

BEGINNING TO WRITE a biography of Abraham Lincoln in 1922, former U. S. Senator Albert J. Beveridge denied that the "last word" on Lincoln had already been written by arguing that "the first word has not been penned." Beveridge's own Lincoln, meticulously researched and lavishly footnoted, completed only through 1858 when Beveridge died, did not achieve status as a "last word" but instead took a place of honor in the Lincoln literature. Today Lincoln books emerge with ever-greater frequency. Somehow every generation must discover Lincoln anew.

Gigantic disparities exist between this enormous Lincoln literature and individual reality. Sometimes the greatest of all Americans becomes a screen upon which flicker the fantasies of his fellow citizens. Most thoughtful Americans come to terms with Lincoln, either quickly, through a single experience with a book or a television production, or slowly, through immersion in that vast literature.

Frank Williams has never been satisfied with easy answers about a man who has always loomed so large in his life. He has been a Lincoln collector since childhood. His massive Lincoln collection, in addition to familiar books and pamphlets, includes microfilm of original sources. As a young man, he became a key participant in the Lincoln industry, beginning with the Lincoln Group of Boston and later embracing every major Lincoln organization in the country. Eventually he ripened as an expert, appearing before any group willing to listen to a speech about Lincoln.

The qualities that raise these essays to first rank rest in their author. In addition to his immersion in the Lincoln literature, he brings to them long experience in the law, both as a lawyer (his quarter century of practice parallels that of Lincoln) and now as a judge. Unlike Lincoln, who entered the White House with a deficiency of administrative experience, Judge Williams has long been adept at leadership in many areas. Lincoln's antebellum military experience was something that he ridiculed for political purposes; Judge Williams is proud of his role as tank commander. Lincoln's reading rarely extended beyond contemporary politics and law, while Judge Williams reads omnivorously. Accordingly, Williams brings a variety of experiences and perspectives to these Lincoln essays.

Unlike many authors in the Lincoln field, Williams has been responsive to criticism and suggestion. Like Beveridge, he has a wide circle of friends in the historical community whom he calls upon for assistance. Other authorities have refined the thought, and editorial suggestions have prompted revision. These are polished presentations, in which he and his friends can take pride.

Readers have now had the pleasure of an anthology of Frank Williams's best. To have heard them as originally presented would have required attending many Lincoln group banquets, and Judge Williams, a remarkable cook among other achievements, would be the first to recommend the typeset experience.

John Y. Simon
Executive Director
Ulysses S. Grant Association
Southern Illinois University
Carbondale, Illinois

Bibliography

Index

Bibliography

Aaron, Daniel. "What Can You Learn from a Historical Novel?" *American Heritage Magazine,* October 1992, 56.

Abbott, Philip. "Prudent Archery: FDR's Lincoln." In *Abraham Lincoln: Contemporary,* ed. Frank J. Williams and William D. Pederson, 22–34. Campbell, Calif.: Savas Woodbury, 1995.

Allen, Woody. *The Query.* In *Side Effects,* 113–21. New York: Random House, 1980.

Alley, John B. *Reminiscences of Abraham Lincoln.* Edited by Allen Thorndike Rice. New York: North American Review, 1888.

Ambrose, Stephen E. *Halleck: Lincoln's Chief of Staff.* Baton Rouge: Louisiana State University Press, 1962.

Angle, Paul, ed. *Herndon's Life of Lincoln.* Greenwich, Conn.: Fawcett, 1961.

Arnold, Isaac N. *The Life of Abraham Lincoln.* 11th ed. Chicago: Jansen, McClurg, 1909.

Athearn, Robert G., ed. *Soldier in the West: The Civil War Letters of Alfred Lacy Hough.* Philadelphia: University of Pennsylvania Press, 1957.

Bailey, Thomas A. *Presidential Greatness.* New York: Irvington, 1978.

Baker, George E., ed. *Works of William H. Seward.* 5 vols. Boston: Houghton Mifflin, 1884.

Bacon, Georgianna Woolsey, and Eliza Woolsey Harland, comps. *Letters of a Family During the War for the Union, 1861–1862.* 2 vols. N.p., 1899.

Beale, Howard K., ed. *Diary of Gideon Welles, Secretary of the Navy Under Lincoln and Johnson.* 3 vols. New York: Norton, 1960.

Bennett, Lerone, Jr. *Forced into Glory: Abraham Lincoln's White Dream.* Chicago: Johnson, 2000.

———. "Was Abe Lincoln a White Supremacist?" *Ebony,* February 1968, 35–42.

Biographical Dictionary of the United States Congress, 1774–1989. Bicentennial ed. Washington, D.C.: Government Printing Office, 1989.

Blaine, James G. *Twenty Years of Congress: From Lincoln to Garfield.* 2 vols. Norwich, Conn.: Henry Bill, 1884.

Bibliography

Bly, Robert. "What the Mayans Could Teach the Joint Chiefs." *New York Times,* July 23, 1993, sec. S, 27.

Boritt, Gabor S. "'Unfinished Work': Lincoln, Meade, and Gettysburg." In *Lincoln's Generals,* ed. Gabor Boritt. New York: Oxford University Press, 1994.

Brinkley, Alan. "The 43 Percent President." *New York Times Magazine,* July 4, 1993, 23.

Brooks, Noah. *Washington in Lincoln's Time.* Edited by Herbert Mitgang. New York: Rinehart, 1958.

Brown, Dennis (adapted from Mary Raymond Shipman Andrews). *The Perfect Tribute.* American Broadcasting Corporation, April 21, 1992.

Bruce, Robert V. "Lincoln and the Riddle of Death." Fourth Annual R. Gerald McMurtry Lecture. Fort Wayne, Ind.: Louis A. Warren Lincoln Library and Museum, 1981.

Buckley, William F., Jr. "By George, Spare Us the Presumption of This Scatter-Minded Southern Statest." *Providence Sunday Journal,* November 1, 1992.

Burke, Edmund, Ross J. S. Hoffman, and Paul Levack, eds. *Burke's Politics: Selected Writings and Speeches of Edmund Burke.* New York: Knopf, 1949.

Burns, James MacGregor. *Leadership.* New York: Harper and Row, 1978.

Carter, Robert Goldthwaite. *Four Brothers in Blue; or, Sunshine and Shadows of the War of the Rebellion.* Austin: University of Texas Press, 1978.

Catton, Bruce. *Grant Takes Command.* Boston: Little, Brown, 1969.

Chandler, William. *The Soldier's Right to Vote. Who Opposes It? Who Favors It? Or the Record of the McClellan Copperheads Against Allowing the Soldier Who Fights, the Right to Vote While Fighting.* Washington: L. Towers, 1864.

Charmley, John. *Churchill: The End of Glory.* New York: Harcourt, Brace, 1993.

Churchill, Winston S. *The Second World War.* 6 vols. Boston: Houghton Mifflin, 1949.

Civil War Miscellaneous Collection. U.S. Army Military History Institute, Carlisle Barracks, Pa.

Clift, Eleanor. "Testing Ground: The Inside Story of How Clinton Survived the Campaign's Worst Moments." *Newsweek,* March 30, 1992, 35.

Coddington, Edwin B. *The Gettysburg Campaign: A Study in Command.* New York: Scribner's, 1968.

Coffin, Charles Carleton. *The Boys of '61; on Four Years of Fighting: Personal Observation with the Army and Navy, from the First Battle of Bull Run to the Fall of Richmond.* Boston, 1885.

Colville, John. *The Fringes of Power: 10 Downing Street Diaries, 1939–1955.* London: Norton, 1985.

Cox, Florence, ed. *Kiss Josey for Me!* Santa Ana, Calif.: Friis-Pioneer Press, 1974.

Bibliography

Cox, LaWanda, and John H. Cox. *Politics, Principle, and Prejudice, 1865–1866.* New York: Free Press, 1963.

Cox, Samuel S. *Eight Years in Congress from 1857–1865.* New York: D. Appleton, 1865.

———. Papers. John Hay Library, Brown University.

———. *Union, Disunion, Reunion: Three Decades of Federal Legislation, 1855–1885.* Providence, R.I.: J. A. and R. A. Reid, 1885.

Cullom, Shelby M. *Fifty Years of Public Service.* Chicago: A. C. McClurg, 1911.

Cuomo, Mario M., and Harold Holzer. "Lincoln's Second Inaugural Address," presented at the New York Historical Society, June 11–July 19, 1992.

———, eds. *Lincoln on Democracy.* New York: HarperCollins, 1990.

Current, Richard Nelson. *The Lincoln Nobody Knows.* New York: McGraw-Hill, 1958.

Dana, Charles A. *Recollections of the Civil War.* New York: D. Appleton, 1898.

Davies, James C. *Human Nature in Politics.* New York: Wiley, 1963.

Davis, William C. *Lincoln's Men: How President Lincoln Became Father to an Army and a Nation.* New York. Free Press, 1999

Davis, William V. *Robert Bly: The Poet and His Critics.* Columbia: Camden House, 1994.

Dawes, Rufus. *Service with the Sixth Wisconsin Volunteers.* Dayton: Morningside Press, 1984.

Dennett, Tyler, ed. *Lincoln and the Civil War in the Diaries and Letters of John Hay.* New York: Dodd, Mead, 1939.

Dexter, Beatrice. "Abraham Lincoln's Corpse Revived." *Weekly World News,* October 5, 1993, 4–5.

Dixon, Norman. *On the Psychology of Military Incompetence.* London: Jonathan Cape, 1976

Donald, David "Getting Right with Lincoln." In *Lincoln Reconsidered: Essays on the Civil War Era,* 2d ed., 3–18. New York: Vintage Books, 1989.

———. *Lincoln.* New York: Simon and Schuster, 1995.

Drake, Julia A., ed. *The Mail Goes Through; or, The Civil War Letters of George Drake.* San Angelo, Tex.: Anchor, 1964.

Duff, John J. *Abraham Lincoln, Prairie Lawyer.* New York: Rinehart, 1960.

Dunn, William E. Papers, *Civil War Times Illustrated* Collection.

Duram, James C., and Eleanor A. Duram, eds. *Soldier of the Cross: The Civil War Diary and Correspondence of Rev. Andrew Jackson Hartstock.* Manhattan, Kans.: Military Affairs/Aerospace Historian, 1979.

Ellis, Thomas T. *Leaves from the Diary of an Army Surgeon.* New York: J. Bradburn, 1863.

Bibliography

Engert, Roderick M., ed. *Maine to the Wilderness: The Civil War Letters of Private William Lawson, 20th Maine Infantry.* Orange, Va.: North South Trader, 1993.

Fehrenbacher, Don E. *The Changing Image of Lincoln in American Historiography.* Oxford: Clarendon Press, 1968.

———. "The Paradoxes of Freedom." In *Lincoln in Text and Context: Collected Essays.* Stanford: Stanford University Press, 1987.

Fehrenbacher, Don E., and Virginia Fehrenbacher, eds. *Recollected Words of Abraham Lincoln.* Stanford: Stanford University Press, 1996.

Fields, Barbara J. "Who Freed the Slaves?" In *The Civil War: An Illustrated History,* ed. Geoffrey C. Ward, Ric Burns, and Ken Burns, 178–81. New York: Knopf, 1990.

Flynn, Edward J. *You're the Boss.* Westport, Conn.: Greenwood, 1983.

Franklin, John Hope. "The Emancipation Proclamation: An Act of Justice." *Prologue: Quarterly of the National Archives* 5 (summer 1993): 151–53.

Freidel, Frank B. *Franklin D. Roosevelt: A Rendezvous with Destiny.* Boston: Little, Brown, 1990.

———. *Union Pamphlets of the Civil War, 1961–1865.* Cambridge: Harvard University Press, 1967.

Fry, James B. In *Reminiscences of Abraham Lincoln by Distinguished Men of His Time,* 6th ed., ed. Allen Thorndike Rice, 387–404. New York: North American, 1888.

Garrison, William L., to Helen Garrison, June 9, 11, 1864, William L. Garrison MSS, Boston Public Library.

Gibbon, John. *Personal Recollections of the Civil War.* New York: Putnam, 1928.

Gilbert, Martin. *Winston S. Churchill: Finest Hour, 1939–1941.* London: C and T Publications, 1983.

Gilligan, Carol. *In a Different Voice: Psychological Theory and Women's Development.* Cambridge: Harvard University Press, 1982.

Goodwin, Doris Kearns, and James MacGregor Burns. "True Leadership." In *The Rating Game in American Politics,* ed. William D. Pederson and Ann McLaurin, 213–32. New York: Irvington, 1987.

Gottlieb, Agnes Hoope, Henry Gottlieb, Barbara Bowers, and Brent Bowers. *1,000 Years, 1,000 People: Ranking the Men and Women Who Shaped the Millennium.* New York: Kodansha International, 1998.

Greene, A. Wilson. "Meade's Pursuit of Lee from Gettysburg to Falling Waters." In *The Third Day at Gettysburg and Beyond,* ed. Gary W. Gallagher. Chapel Hill: University of North Carolina Press, 1994.

Greenleaf, Margery, ed. *Letters to Eliza from a Union Soldier, 1862–1865.* Chicago: Follett, 1970.

Bibliography

Greenstein, Fred I. "What the President Means to Americans." In *Choosing the President,* ed. James David Barber, 121–47. Englewood Cliffs, N.J.: Prentice-Hall, 1974.

Grigg, John. "Churchill and Lloyd George." In *Churchill: A Major New Assessment of His Life in Peace and War,* ed. Robert Blake and William Roger Louis. New York: Norton, 1993.

Gurganus, Allan. *The Oldest Living Confederate Widow Tells All.* New York: Ballantine, 1988.

Halleck, Henry Wager. *Elements of Military Art and Science.* 2d ed. New York, 1861.

Haupt, Herman. *Reminiscences of General Herman Haupt.* Milwaukee: Wright and Joys, 1901.

Hearn, Chester G. *Six Years of Hell: Harpers Ferry During the Civil War.* Baton Rouge: Louisiana State University Press, 1996.

Henderson, Harold. "Lincoln's Death and Transfiguration." *Illinois Times,* February 10–16, 1983, 6.

Hofstadter, Richard. *The American Political Tradition.* New York: Vintage Books, 1974.

Holzer, Harold. *The Lincoln-Douglas Debates: The First Unexpurgated Text.* New York: HarperCollins, 1995.

Horan, James. *The Pinkertons: The Detective Dynasty That Made History.* New York: Crown, 1967.

Hughes, Robert. *Culture of Complaint: The Fraying of America.* New York: Oxford University Press, 1993.

Julian, George W. *Political Recollections, 1840 to 1872.* Chicago: Jansen McClurg, 1884.

Kammen, Michael. "Changing Presidential Perspectives on the American Past." *Prologue Quarterly of the National Archives* 25 (spring 1993): 48–59.

Kauffman, Henry, to Katherine Kreitzer, October 15, 1864. In *The Civil War Letters (1862–1865) of Private Henry Kauffman,* ed. David McCordick. Lewiston, N.Y.: Edward Mellen Press, 1991.

Keegan, John. "Churchill's Strategy." In *Churchill: A Major New Assessment of His Life in Peace and War,* ed. Robert Blake and William Roger Louis. New York: Norton, 1993.

Kent, Arthur A., ed. *Three Years with Company K.* Rutherford, N.J.: Associated University Presses, 1976.

Klement, Frank L. *The Limits of Dissent: Clement L. Vallandigham and the Civil War.* New York: Fordham University Press.

Kunhardt III, Philip B., and Philip B. Kunhardt Jr. *Lincoln.* Capital Cities/American Broadcasting Corporation, December 26 and 27, 1992.

Bibliography

Lamolinara, Gary. "I Do Solemnly Swear . . . : L.C. Exhibition Chronicles an American Political Tradition." *Library of Congress Information Bulletin,* January 25, 1993, 30–37.

Lamon, Ward Hill. *Recollections of Abraham Lincoln, 1847–1865.* 2d ed. Edited by Dorothy Lamon Teillard. Washington, D.C., 1911. Introduction to University of Nebraska, Bison Book ed., 1994, by James A. Rawley.

Larrabee, Eric. *Commander in Chief: Franklin Delano Roosevelt, His Lieutenants, and Their War.* New York: Simon and Schuster, 1987.

Latham, R. W., to William Henry Seward, January 9, 1865. William Henry Seward MSS, Rush Rhees Seward Library, University of Rochester.

Lincoln, Abraham. *The Collected Works of Abraham Lincoln.* 9 vols. Edited by Roy P. Basler, Marion Dolores Pratt, and Lloyd A. Dunlap. New Brunswick, N.J.: Rutgers University Press, 1953–55.

Lincoln Legal Papers Project, Illinois State Historical Library, Springfield.

Lindsey, David. *"Sunset" Cox, Irrepressible Democrat.* Detroit: Wayne State University Press, 1959.

Long, David E. *The Jewel of Liberty: Abraham Lincoln's Reelection and the End of Slavery.* Mechanicsburg, Pa.: Stackpole Books, 1994.

Lowenstein, Jerald M., in Frank J. Williams, "Lincolniana in 1992." *Journal of the Abraham Lincoln Association* 14 (summer 1993): 96–97.

Lowry, Thomas P. *Don't Shoot That Boy! Abraham Lincoln and Military Justice.* Mason City, Iowa: Savas, 1999.

Marvel, William. *Burnside.* Chapel Hill: University of North Carolina Press, 1991.

McCullough, David. *Truman.* New York: Simon and Schuster, 1992.

McMurtry, Gerald R. "Lincoln Need Not Have Signed the Resolution Submitting the Thirteenth Amendment to the United States." *Lincoln Lore* 1604, October 1971, 1.

McPherson, Edward. *The Political History of the United States or America During the Great Rebellion.* New York, 1864.

McPherson, James M. Preface. *Abraham Lincoln and the Second American Revolution.* New York: Oxford University Press, 1990.

———. *Battle Cry of Freedom: The Civil War Era.* New York: Oxford University Press, 1988.

———. *Who Freed the Slaves? Lincoln and Emancipation.* Redlands: Lincoln Memorial Shrine, 1993.

McSweeney, Samuel T. "Re-Electing Lincoln: The Union Party Campaign and the Military Vote in Connecticut." *Civil War History* 32 (June 1986): 2.

Meade, George. *The Life and Letters of George Gordon Meade.* 2 vols. New York: Scribner's, 1913.

Miers, Earl Schenck, ed. *Lincoln Day by Day: A Chronology, 1809–1865.* 3 vols. Washington: Lincoln Sesquicentennial Commission, 1960.

Mitgang, Herbert. "Abraham Lincoln: Friend of a Free Press." *Sino-American Relations: An International Quarterly* 18 (spring 1992): 106.

———. "Reagan's 'Lincoln' Quotation Disputed." "Erratum," *New York Times,* August 19, 1992, A13.

Morgan, Edwin, to Edwin McMasters Stanton, September 15, 1864. Stanton Papers, Library of Congress.

Murray, Robert K., and Tim H. Blessing. "The Presidential Performance Study: A Progress Report." *Journal of American History* 70, no. 3 (December 1983): 535–55.

Neely, Mark E., Jr. *The Fate of Liberty: Abraham Lincoln and Civil Liberties.* New York: Oxford University Press, 1991.

———. "Lincoln and the Theory of Self-Emancipation." In *The Continuing Civil War: Essays in Honor of the Civil War Round Table of Chicago,* ed. John Y. Simon and Barbara Hughett, 45–59. Dayton: Morningside Press, 1992.

Nevins, Allan, ed. *A Diary of Battle: The Personal Journals of Colonel Charles S. Wainwright, 1861–1865.* New York: Da Capo, 1998.

Nicolay, John G., and John Hay. *Abraham Lincoln: A History.* 10 vols. New York: Century, 1890.

Noe, Kenneth W., ed. *A Southern Boy in Blue: The Memoir of Marcus Woodcock, 9th Kentucky Infantry (USA).* Knoxville: University of Tennessee Press, 1996.

Noonan, John T., Jr. *Bribes.* New York: Macmillan, 1984.

Oates, Stephen B. *With Malice Toward None: The Life of Abraham Lincoln.* New York: New American Library, 1978.

Ostendorf, Lloyd, and Walter Olesky, eds. *Lincoln's Unknown Private Life: An Oral History by His Black Housekeeper, Mariah Vance, 1850–1860.* Mamaroneck, N.Y.: Hastings, 1995.

Paludan, Phillip Shaw. *The Presidency of Abraham Lincoln.* Lawrence: University Press of Kansas, 1994.

Papers of the Military Historical Society of Massachusetts. 14 vols., 1881–1918, reprint, Wilmington, 1989–90.

Pederson, William D., and Ann McLaurin, eds. *The Rating Game in American Politics.* New York: Irvington, 1978.

Peterson, Merrill. *Lincoln in American Memory.* New York: Oxford University Press 1994.

Pomeroy, Earl S. "Lincoln, the Thirteenth Amendment, and the Admission of Nevada." *Pacific Historical Review* 12 (1943): 362–68.

Porter, Horace. *Campaigning with Grant.* New York: Century, 1897.

Randall, James G. *Constitutional Problems Under Lincoln.* Rev. ed. Urbana: University of Illinois Press, 1951.

―――. "The Rule of Law Under Lincoln." *Lincoln, the Liberal Statesman.* New York: Dodd, Mead, 1947.

―――. "Vindictives and Vindication." In *Mr. Lincoln,* ed. Richard N. Current, 317–40. New York: Dodd, Mead, 1957.

Reilley, George Love Anthony. "The Camden and Amboy Railroad in New Jersey Politics, 1830–1871." Ph.D. diss., Columbia University, 1951.

Rhodes, James Ford. *History of the United States from the Compromise of 1850.* 7 vols. New York: Macmillan, 1892.

Rice, Allen Thorndike, ed. *Reminiscences of Abraham Lincoln by Distinguished Men of His Times.* New York: North American Review, 1888.

Riddle, Albert Gallatin. *Recollections of War Times.* New York: Putnam, 1892.

Sandburg, Carl. *Abraham Lincoln: The Prairie Years,* vols. 1 and 2. New York: Harcourt, Brace, 1926.

Schell, Jonathan. "Union Divides Lincoln and Gorbachev." "Viewpoints." *Newsday,* November 21, 1991, 127.

Schlesinger, Arthur M., Jr. "The History of Those Words Lincoln Never Said." *Washington Post,* August 28, 1992, A23.

―――. "The Ultimate Approval Rating." *New York Times Magazine,* December 15, 1996, 46–51.

Schuyler, Robert Livingston, ed. *Frederic William Maitland, Historian: Selections from His Writings.* Berkeley: University of California Press, 1960.

Scovel, James M. "Thaddeus Stevens." *Lippincott's Monthly Magazine* 61 (1898): 550.

Sears, Stephen W., ed. *The Civil War Papers of George B. McClellan: Selected Correspondence, 1860–1865.* New York: Ticknor and Fields, 1989.

Sedgwick, Henry Dwight. *Francis Parkman.* Boston: Houghton Mifflin, 1904.

Shogan, Robert. *Hard Bargain: How FDR Twisted Churchill's Arm, Evaded the Law, and Changed the Role of the American Presidency.* New York: Scribner's, 1995.

Simon, John Y., ed. *The Papers of Ulysses S. Grant.* 22 vols. Carbondale: Southern Illinois University Press, 1984.

Speed, Joshua F. *Reminiscences of Abraham Lincoln and Notes of a Visit to California: Two Lectures.* Louisville, Ky.: John P. Morton, 1884.

Stevenson, James A. "American Voyages of Lincoln and Huck Finn." *Lincoln Herald* 90, no. 4 (winter 1988): 130–33.

Stevenson, Richard W. "C. Northcote Parkinson, Eighty-three, Dies; Writer with a Wry View of Labor." *New York Times,* March 12, 1993.

Bibliography

Sunderland, Glenn W. *Five Days to Glory.* South Brunswick, N.J.: A. S. Barnes, 1970.

Tarbell, Ida M. *The Early Life of Abraham Lincoln.* New York: S. S. McClure, 1896.

———. *A Reporter for Lincoln: The Story of Henry E. Wing, Soldier and Newspaperman.* New York: Macmillan, 1927.

Taylor, A. J. P. "The Statesman." In *Churchill Revised: A Critical Assessment.* New York: Dial Press, 1969.

———. *The War Lords.* New York: Atheneum, 1978.

Thomas, Benjamin P., and Harold M. Hyman. *Stanton: The Life and Times of Lincoln's Secretary of War.* 1962; reprint, Westport, Conn.: Greenwood Press, 1980.

Thorndike, Rachel S., ed. *The Sherman Letters.* New York: Scribner, 1894.

Tullai, Martin D. "Mr. Bush Tries Out Abe-Speak." *San Jose Mercury News,* February 12, 1992.

———. "The Precedent for Dumping a V.P." *Baltimore Evening Sun,* January 7, 1992.

U.S. Statutes at Large. Vol. 1 (1848); vol. 10 (1853).

Vallandigham, James Laird. *A Life of Clement L. Vallandigham.* Baltimore: Turnbull, 1872.

Vidal, Gore. *Screening History.* Cambridge: Harvard University Press, 1992.

Villard, Oswald. *Fighting Years: Memoir of a Liberal Editor.* New York: Harcourt, Brace, 1939.

Vorenberg, Michael. *Final Freedom: The Civil War, the Abolition of Slavery, and the Thirteenth Amendment.* New York: Cambridge University Press, 2001.

The War of the Rebellion: A Compilation of the Official Records of the Union and Confederate Armies. 128 vols. Washington, D.C.: Government Printing Office, 1880–1901.

Waters, Harry F. "Lincoln Reconstructed." *Newsweek,* December 28, 1992, 61.

Weems, Mason Locke. *The Life of Washington.* Edited by Marcus Cunliffe. 1809; rpt., Cleveland: World, 1965.

Welles, Gideon. *The Diary of Gideon Welles.* Edited by Howard K. Beale. 3 vols. New York: Norton, 1960.

———. *Lincoln and Seward.* New York: Sheldon, 1960.

Williams, Frank J. "Lincolniana in 1991." *Journal of the Abraham Lincoln Association* 13 (summer 1992): 94.

Williams, Frank J., William D. Pederson, and Vincent J. Marsala, eds. *Abraham Lincoln: Sources and Style of Leadership.* Westport, Conn.: Greenwood, 1994.

Williams, T. Harry. *Lincoln and His Generals.* New York: Knopf, 1952.

Willing, Richard. "Clinton Leans on 'Honest Abe.'" *Detroit News,* September 27, 1992, 1B.

Wills, Garry. *Certain Trumpets: The Call of Leaders.* New York: Simon and Schuster, 1994.

————. *Cincinnatus: George Washington and the Enlightenment.* Garden City, N.Y.: Doubleday, 1984.

————. "Dishonest Abe." *Time,* October 5, 1992, 42.

Wilson, James H. *Under the Old Flag.* 2 vols. New York: Appleton, 1912.

Zall, P. M., ed. *Abe Lincoln Laughing: Humorous Anecdotes from Original Sources by and about Abraham Lincoln.* Knoxville: University of Tennessee Press, 1955.

Zebrowski, Carl. Interview. "Why the South Lost the Civil War." *American History,* October 1995.

Index

Page numbers in italics direct the reader to illustrations.

Index

Index

Index

Index

Index

Index

EX LIBRIS

A. Lincoln

FRANK & VIRGINIA WILLIAMS
COLLECTION OF
LINCOLNIANA

Frank J. Williams is chief justice of the Supreme Court of Rhode Island and a well-known expert on Abraham Lincoln. He has authored, coauthored, or coedited nine books, contributed chapters to several others, and lectured on the subject throughout the country. He has also amassed, with his wife, Virginia, a private library and archive that rank among the nation's largest and finest Lincoln collections. In 2000, the chief justice was appointed to the United States Abraham Lincoln Bicentennial Commission created by Congress to plan events to commemorate the two hundredth birthday of Abraham Lincoln in 2009. Since 1996, Williams has served as the founding chairman of the Lincoln Forum, a national assembly of Lincoln and Civil War devotees. He served for nine years as president of the Abraham Lincoln Association and for fourteen years as president of the Lincoln Group of Boston. He is currently at work on a bibliography of all the Lincoln titles published since 1865 and, with Harold Holzer and Edna Greene Medford, is writing a book on the Emancipation.